PORTRAIT OF A CHRISTIAN LEADER

Developing Skills for Maximum Impact

✠ ✠ ✠

TERRY KING

PORTRAIT OF A CHRISTIAN LEADER
DEVELOPING SKILLS FOR MAXIMUM IMPACT

Copyright © 2020 Terry King
All rights reserved.

All scripture quotations, unless otherwise noted, are taken from the Holy Bible, New International Version®, NIV®. Copyright © 1973, 1978, 1984, 2011 by Biblica, Inc. ™ Used by permission of Zondervan. All rights reserved worldwide. www.zondervan.com. The "NIV" and "New International Version" are trademarks registered in the United States Patent and Trademark Office by Biblica, Inc.™

Scripture quotations marked (NASB) taken from the New American Standard Bible®, Copyright © 1960, 1962, 1963, 1968, 1971, 1972, 1973, 1975, 1977, 1995 by The Lockman Foundation. Used by permission.

ISBN 978-1-7370995-0-5

ACKNOWLEDGEMENTS

I have to start by thanking the greatest blessing in my life, my wife, Alisa. Your countless words of encouragement kept me moving forward when I was ready to quit. You are an inspiration to me.

Many thanks to our dear partners at Rock Solid Solutions – Todd and Amy Goetz – for your seemingly endless hours of processing, dreaming, and your enduring, "What do you think about this?" questions. Looks like we did it and we have only just begun.

I am also thankful to Yvonne and Mark Walters, and their willingness to believe this project could be done. Your support so many years ago is still providing the momentum to see this through.

To all of our other family and friends who listened, shared our burdens, and prayed. This is tribute to true friends and family who stay the course and never give up.

And finally, to every Christian leader, may this book inspire you to think outside-the-box and spend your life of influence sharing Christ with those in the workplace in tangible ways. Form teams, dream dreams, and cast a big vision for the next generation of leaders to follow Him.

CONTENTS

Introduction 9

Chapter 1: Servant Leader 13

    Biblical Perspective 13

    Action vs. Attitude 15

    A Mirror Image 18

Chapter 2: Spiritual Leader 23

    Character Development 23

    Influence and Spirituality 26

    Reading and Writing 30

Chapter 3: Missional Leader 35

    Organizational Mission 35

    Organizational Structure 38

    Communicating/Responding to the Mission 41

    Increasing Employee Involvement 44

Chapter 4: Evidence-Based Leader 51

Research is Imperative 51

No More Assumptions 54

Taking Time—Now or Later 57

Chapter 5: Team Leader 61

Organizational Fit 61

Job Fit 64

Diagnosing Problems and Motivational Issues 68

Developing a Measurable Leader/Follower Plan ..73

Chapter 6: Communicating Leader 79

Evaluating Communication Styles 80

Knowing What Your Team Wants and Needs 86

Analyzing Organizational Conflict 90

Chapter 7: Change Leader 95

Revolutionary and Evolutionary Change 97

Identifying Success and Failure
in Organizational Change 103

Strategic Thinking 105

Strategic Planning 108

Chapter 8: Innovating Leader 113

Evidence-Based Innovation 115

Diagnosing Innovation Issues 117

Using Innovation to Improve Organizations 123

Chapter 9: Coaching Leader 129

Coaching Leaders 132

Establishing Trust 134

Maintaining Integrity 136

Building a Model for Christian Leadership Coaching 138

Why Accountability is Important 144

Chapter 10: Initiating Leader 149

Understanding Your Role as a Christian Leader 150

Developing Those Under You 152

From Daydreams to Realization 154

Vulnerability 157

Chapter 11: A Final Challenge 161

Start Now 161

Accountability Team 163

Self-Evaluation 165

Your Final Chapter 169

References 171

Introduction

One of my favorite pastimes as a child was to look through one of several old, dusty boxes of family pictures. My sisters and I would pull out each photo and recall names and places known only to Mom and Dad but shared with us over the years. In those moments, we would laugh at the expressions of long-lost family members whose stories we never knew. Each face, each place, each name represented someone whose life intersected with us or our parents somewhere in the past. Those pictures could never adequately tell the story of those individuals; they were only snapshots—one moment in their life.

If we were fortunate enough to have Mom or Dad join us as we looked through those pictures, they would fill in details, and suddenly those snapshots would begin to breathe. This wasn't just the smiling face of a young military man; this was a third cousin, who lived just down the road from my mom when she was a child. They would walk to school together and share water from the same creek. The picture of this young man would tell a story if we had someone to fill in the details. The snapshots of our lives tell stories too. If we take the time to weave them into a scrapbook, those single pictures tell the story of our lives.

This book offers snapshots of a leader's life as well. Woven together, they present a complete picture of a leader who is following and modeling Christ. Take one of these snapshots away and the leader is incomplete; however, that is not to say this book represents an exhaustive list. I have intentionally left out the characteristics that should be a part of every Christian's life (love, joy, peace, patience, etc.) and included those that have often been lost from modern-day leadership development.

These snapshots should tell the story of every Christian leader's life. By taking the time to consider, nurture, and further develop them, you will soon discover you are writing the chapters of your life, creating a scrapbook of your own Christian leadership journey—one snapshot at a time.

Much of this book is written from the perspective of a Christian leader serving in a larger organization. As such, the individual who works alone or who owns/serves in a smaller company, church, or non-profit may feel like the insights might not work for their situation. If you find yourself among this group, trust me that these titles and topics are still relevant for your situation. Much of my own leadership experience was in serving a smaller church or working in smaller organizations.

After completing a graduate degree in organizational leadership in 2010, I launched my own leadership and organizational coaching business in 2013. As a result of that, I have been able to share many of these leadership insights with business and ministry leaders as well as with organizational teams and non-profit boards. Adding this book to your leadership toolbox will serve you well regardless of the career or ministry track you are on.

Working solo or in a smaller company only means you will need to exercise some additional creativity to build the teams I suggest or to find ways to make these concepts become a reality. You can always pull people in from outside your organization or church to put together the suggested teams. You can include family and friends who will stoke the fires of your creativity. Until He brings others around you in your journey, be creative and watch what He will do.

Portrait of a Christian Leader

This book will help you understand how to become the leader He wants you to be. At the end of each chapter, you will find a few ways to develop that leadership trait in your own life and in the lives of those you serve. In addition, I encourage you to follow the link and use the workbook that compliments this book. I trust this adventure will enlighten you, challenge you, and help you look more like Jesus Christ as you continue your journey toward Him.

CHAPTER 1 Servant Leader

Biblical Perspective

"... the great leader is seen as servant first, and that simple fact is the key to his greatness." [1]

The concept of servant-leadership has long been lauded by many Christian leaders. Leadership gurus have told us that to look like Jesus, we must become servant leaders. It is most unfortunate that few of them have walked through the process by which that transformation takes place.

Reality check—servant leadership is not normal. It goes against our human nature to serve others first. It is not natural to focus on serving the needs of others before you consider your own needs. Thus, it is necessary to learn this process and invest yourself in seeing it through. To be a great Christian leader, you must learn to serve, and as ironic as it seems, becoming a servant leader is less about serving than you may think.

When explaining servant leadership, an overwhelming number of Christian leadership experts choose to focus on John 13, where Jesus washes the feet of the disciples. The Bible declares that Jesus "... loved them to the end" (John 13:1). As a result of this act, many focus on the act of washing feet as Jesus's supreme act of servant leadership. Conferences have been developed, books have been written, and some denominations have included this among the ordinances of their church. The purpose here is not to belittle the action of those who do this but to ask everyone to put the brakes on for a moment.

If becoming a servant leader was all about washing feet, the church could have (and should have) perfected it long ago. Developing hands-on seminars where feet are washed with scented soap from Jerusalem and where towels made from Middle Eastern cotton would be the norm for becoming a servant leader. But servant leadership cannot be commercialized, neatly packaged, or easily accommodated. It is difficult, it is painful, and it is not easily accomplished. As anyone who has had their feet washed by someone else can attest, it is a transforming act for both parties.

I am under the impression that Jesus's act of servant leadership is far more than the outward act of washing feet. If leaders are only interested in performing outward acts to be seen and experienced by others to elevate their standing, there are abundant opportunities to accomplish that. When a leader "washes feet," sends a card, or recognizes a subordinate in public, servant leadership is not necessarily taking place. If I perform in any fashion for others to see it, my reward will come from man and not God. I am not advocating servant leadership be secretive either. It is quite difficult to wash feet unknowingly.

Action vs. Attitude

True servant leadership finds its roots not in the public washing of feet but in the attitude that prevails before the basin and towel are ever acquired. For all the things Christians have deduced from the life of Christ (from proving our humility by driving rusted-out cars to proving our worthiness by driving the most expensive cars), we have often left out a most profound nugget—servant leadership is more about attitude than about action.

Paul encourages us to develop the attitude of Christ in Philippians 2:5, "Have this attitude in yourselves which was also in Christ Jesus" (NASB). You can perform outward acts like washing feet, standing by a friend in a time of adversity, and even performing random acts of kindness and never be a servant leader. We can discipline ourselves to "look good" in the eyes of those around us, but that is not leadership nor servanthood.

The plain truth is this: servant leadership is always about your attitude, your leadership, *and* your service toward others. For too long, we have made it all about service. We have been taught to believe that if we are serving others, we are servant leaders. Consequently, we have a generation of leaders who are convinced they look like Jesus but who are more concerned about what people think than what Jesus thinks. If you want to look like Jesus, you must do more than wash feet. You must invest in an attitude of service to those under you. If your subordinates feel loved, cared for, and nurtured, it will not be because you literally cleaned their feet. It will be because you have invested in a lifetime of attitude adjustment because those around you experience Him in your words, your actions, *and* your attitude.

Servant leadership is also a top down process. The examples of servant leadership modeled in the life of Christ were always expressed to those He was leading. In this case, it can be reduced to this question: "Do those around me feel like they are being served by me?" Some leaders have been so duped by their own failing leadership styles that they could never honestly answer that question. The only way to know for sure is to ask those under your leadership if they feel served by you. It has been stated by many others that "perception is reality." If your direct reports do not perceive that you care, you are not a very good servant leader. I know it is easy to dismiss some subordinates as having an attitude, but for a leader to dismiss them is to offer an assessment of one's own leadership.

When Jesus served others, people genuinely felt cared for because He genuinely cared. When Jesus encountered the Samaritan woman at the well in John 4, His words were a bit hard, but she experienced freedom as a result of His willingness to serve her in the way she needed. Ultimately, she also felt loved and cared for, and then willingly shared her experience with the other folks in town. He did not serve her in public to draw a crowd. His attitude reflected a genuine love, and that is the heart of servant leadership.

It takes time with Him to temper a hard heart. It takes a bold, honest look at your motives to see if you are truly starting to look like Jesus or just act like Him. When you wash feet and your heart and your hands have the same motivation—to serve as He did without any other purpose than to let the one being served feel loved and cared for—you are on the right track. With practice and discipline, your subordinates may look into your heart, your eyes, and your actions and see Jesus. Those moments are truly rare, but they are worth the wait.

A Mirror Image

If a leader's acts of service look to their own interests first, servant leadership is not being practiced. Servant leadership looks at the needs of others before considering personal needs. Serving others in this way teaches me to die to myself and constantly consider the other person first. This act of service is about them not me.

This is best modeled in the mirror image theory. Everyone is a product of someone else's leadership. No doubt my leadership has left its mark on those I have led. When I did not like what I saw in them, the first step I took was to look inward. When someone begins to work for a servant leader, the servant leader must bear in mind the prevailing attitudes and actions they see are often a result of a previous leader's impact. Good or bad, a worker is often a product of his or her own environment. While the time frame is different for everyone, at some point, that worker will begin to model the characteristics of the leader who is currently influencing him or her. This is what I call the mirror image theory.

If I want to see those who follow me model servant leadership, I must ensure they see it in my leadership first. There have been times in my life that I have not been a very good servant leader. Since first being introduced to Greenleaf's book, *Servant Leadership*, I have always wanted that trait to be a part of who I am. Some days, I succeeded; most years, I did not. When I have seen it modeled in the lives of those I have influenced, I have felt some measure of success. Because I firmly believe in the mirror image theory, I have deduced that my effectiveness as a servant leader leaves much to be desired. Nevertheless, the feeling of success can seldom be matched when one of my subordinates truly begins serving those around him or her.

Are you a real servant leader? Look around you and honestly evaluate those who are experiencing your leadership day in and day out. Those who are relatively new may still be reeling from the leadership of those they recently served under; however, those who have been in their positions for any length of time within your circle of influence will often reflect the model of leadership they see in you. On the surface, most Christian leaders like to think of themselves as servant leaders. They have been taught that because Jesus was a servant leader, they too should be a servant leader. It is unfortunate that most evaluate themselves inaccurately.

Try It!

If you dare, take the time to honestly evaluate your own leadership by working through this list:

1. Am I overly concerned with how others view my outward acts of service?

   _____

   _____

   _____

   _____

   _____

2. Can I serve others without being seen or does my ego drive me to make sure everyone knows what I am doing?

Servant Leader

_____

_____

_____

_____

CHAPTER 2 Spiritual Leader

Character Development

Developing character is not something you can decide to do at some random point in time. The reality is your character has been forming since the day you became aware of your surroundings. The character traits I am nurturing today were seeds that were planted long ago by way of some event, something read, something experienced, or something encountered. The way I saw others react to something caused me to either embrace their reaction or reject it. The result was that good character was being established in my life.

It is difficult to just make a choice one day to be a person of reputable character or to develop character because character has been forming in us through our daily actions.

I can start today to affect my character later in my life, but there is no quick fix to accomplish this task.

I develop character by consistently responding to the life situations and the choices I make over time. The moment we begin making our own decisions, we are developing character. Each resolution I make in my life leaves a mark on me. As I mature, those etchings in my life are the character I have developed. Each conclusion reached will add to the formation of my character, and the character I have developed over time affects the future choices I make. The influence is mutual.

My journey toward developing good character began many years ago. Years of decisions in both major and minor areas of my life have made their mark on me. In the beginning, I made decisions based on personal feelings and ideals. Over time, a picture began to emerge of the most common conclusions for those decisions. Soon there were common trends in the way I drew my conclusions, and this was an indicator of how my character was being developed. As I matured, the patterns of decision-making in my life were the result of the character I was building in my life.

Becoming a man or woman of good reputation and character is no small task. It will require patience and discipline as we sift through the garden of our souls and weed out those things that do not emulate the character of one who walks with Christ. It may require us to spend time searching the life of Jesus to discover the hows and whys of the decisions He made. It may require us to rework the core components of who we are in order to become who we should be. There is no step by step process in order to become a person of character; nevertheless, there is one constant for every person who longs to be known as a man or woman of character—time. I can begin today to change the core of my life, but it will not come easy.

Old ways of thinking, living, and speaking need to be challenged. Routines once held sacred may need to be discarded. Character development is hard work. Nevertheless, as Christian leaders, this is not an investment we can ignore. We owe it our time, effort, sweat, and tears. Who we are at the core, at the root of our lives, will leave an indelible mark on those who we serve and on the cause of Christ at large. What *has been* developed in your life and what *is being* developed in your life are questions worthy of our attention.

Influence and Spirituality

Everyone in a position of leadership is an influencer. The attitude, authenticity, and action you exhibit is and has been influencing those around you. If you see undesirable characteristics in those around you, consider first the measure of influence you have had or have neglected in those individuals. The easiest thing to do in those situations is to point your finger and tell the individual in question he or she has a problem. An authentic person of influence understands his or her impact on the lives of those around them and considers that reality before pointing a finger.

We are people of influence. If a leader is perceived as dishonest or less than genuine, the impact of those traits will be felt throughout the organization. On the other hand, if a leader is perceived as caring, nurturing, and serving, those traits will eventually be experienced throughout the organization as well. Influence moves in both directions, and healthy Christian leaders will never fail to consider their impact on the culture of their workplace. The longer a leader serves one group of people in an organization, the more the group starts to look and act like the leader. Attitudes are contagious! Seeing things that are less than desirable should be a call to look inward, by first examining your own heart and action.

Influence is power. It is the ability to sway a vote, to change an attitude, to make a difference. We see that in the life of Christ. His presence stirred people to the core. For some, that stirring was hatred and disdain for all He represented. For others, that stirring compelled them to leave all they ever knew for something they could not resist. His influence on people, situations, and life conditions compelled others to take notice.

The ability to recognize this characteristic is often lacking in the Christian leaders of the twenty-first century. I could offer speculation as to why this is so, but the root of every reason lies in self. Christian leaders who are consumed with serving themselves seldom recognize their inability to positively influence those around them.

Leaders need to realize that they cannot help but influence others. On good days, bad days, and in-between days, you are influencing those around you. The very nature of the role of a leader equates to influence. Your team will watch your action and reaction to everything from a misplaced order in a local restaurant to major setbacks. Some will watch to criticize; others will watch to learn how they should respond. Leaders influence, and Christian leaders should strive to influence others in a Christ-like manner.

This happens in the way we make decisions, the way we handle ourselves, and the way we relate to those around us. Day-to-day judgments are being made about us based on every part of who we are. If you are in a position of leadership, you are influencing others. How are you handling this responsibility?

While we cannot turn that influence off and on, we can affect how that influence is being meted out, and that is where spirituality comes into play. Every breathing human being on this planet is spiritual. My oldest sister had Down syndrome, and when we started joking and laughing with her, she had a saying that always cut to the chase. Her statement rings loud and true in this discussion too. Our conversations sounded something like this:

> Doris (looks at me and laughs): "What are you saying, old man?"
>
> Terry: "I am not an old man; you are an old woman!"
>
> Doris (laughs): "No, I am not; you are!"

Terry: "You are funny, Doris; you are something else. You are special."

Doris: "I know. God made me that way."

Fewer statements have been truer than the conclusion Doris reached every time—God made me that way! Likewise, we are spiritual because God made us that way. I cannot be un-spiritual. There is part of each of us that will live forever, and that makes us spiritual whether we ever reach that conclusion or not. There are things we can do to enhance our spirituality, and there are things we can do to detract from our spirituality, but we cannot help but be spiritual.

The measure of our spirituality is determined by our connectivity to God. When leaders regularly make decisions that model that of Christ, we can determine that their spirituality is healthy. Likewise, when leaders make decisions that model those things contrary to Christ, we reach the opposite conclusion: their spirituality is not healthy. As a Christian leader, I must model healthy spirituality—there is no other alternative. My team must see Him in me and in my leadership decisions. My identity as a *Christian* leader is distinctly tied to my relationship to Jesus Christ, so to lead in a way that is inconsistent with Jesus could be to label me a non-Christian. That must never be an option, so rule it out now.

The activities that have been traditionally linked to a person's spiritual life are necessary to have a healthy spiritual mind-set. Reading the Bible and spending time in prayer, meditation, worship, etc., all put me in a place of submission to my heavenly Father. To practice them is to draw close to Him. Those activities do not make me spiritual; they heighten my awareness of spiritual things. Making them a regular part of my life will cause the things of this life to be put into proper perspective.

Reading and Writing

These disciplines are basic to our leadership development: a Christian leader needs to be well-read and well-acquainted with writing. Reading reveals the thoughts of others to us, and writing reveals our thoughts to others. Both help to keep a proper perspective and a systematic approach in our growth and ability to lead.

While we may hope that we have progressed as God has purposefully planned, we know that is likely not the case. The books I have read, the discussions I have had with others about the books they have read, and even the books I am planning to read will play a role in the leader I become. I have filed some of the things I have read in the recesses of my mind and others have made their way to the circular file, but they all contribute and will continue to contribute to the leader I become.

Early in my professional development, I made reading a regular part of my lifestyle. I have consumed countless books, some read and re-read; I have processed many and forgotten some. Insights from others have contributed to me as a leader. As a result, they have become a part of my spiritual DNA. Now I am unable to separate the content of those books from my own thoughts and mode of operation because I committed to personally digesting their content. At least in part, I have become the leader I am today based on what I have digested with my eyes.

Just as leadership is partnered with serving, the companion to reading is writing. Writings may consist of notebooks, journals, quotes, and comments; consequently, those documents composed by your own hand are part of the leadership legacy you will leave to others. We as Christian leaders would do well to ask the question, "What will those coming behind me learn from my written journey?"

I recall walking along a path one time in a remote forest off the beaten trail. While there was a path to follow, from time to time it seemed to disappear. After carefully searching, I would pick up the path again only to have the same thing happen repeatedly. It was unfortunate that the path was not clearly marked. I spent so much time trying to find my way, I failed to enjoy the beauty of what was all around me. This is the same thing that happens to those who follow us when we fail to write down our experiences—both positive and negative.

What a gift we could offer others by simply taking the time to communicate our joys, heartaches, and learning experiences along the way. Let those who come behind you learn from your mistakes. Empower them to go further than you—that is the essence of leadership. Write your stories in a journal; jot your thoughts down on napkins, notepads, and cards. Leave no part of your journey undocumented. It not only helps you remember your personal journey and progress; it is also invaluable to those following you.

So, I read, I process, I write. I take the time to document many of my challenges and joys because I want to support the people I am teaching so they avoid the mistakes I made. Some of my ramblings will never make it beyond the paper they are written on. However, others will become the foundation for the thoughts of those coming behind me. With all of that wisdom coming from reading and writing, why would I ever miss this opportunity to leave a legacy?

Try It!

I cannot remember the number of times I responded to a challenge like I am offering you and failed to give a completely honest answer. I wrote things down that I wanted to be the truth or that sounded like the right answer. I wrote things down I wanted others to read about me, but I genuinely want this exercise to be different for you. Do not waste your time lying to yourself here. Record the truth—regardless of what it sounds like. Write it down, and if you decide to share it publicly, people will read what you wrote and perhaps they will be vulnerable enough to be honest about themselves too, and that is when change happens. Genuine change and character development do not happen by accident. They happen most often when we are intentional. That starts today.

Take the time to honestly consider where you are right now.

1. Based on my generalizations of character development, how would those around you rate your character?

   _____

   _____

2. Does your character adequately reflect your relationship with Christ? Why or why not?

   _____

   _____

CHAPTER 3 Missional Leader

Organizational Mission

Fundamentally, each of us has an innate desire to know why. Every parent has experienced the earnest, but incessant "But why?" from their child. It can be fun to experience that every now and again, but after a while, it gets to you. A child will ask that over and over until he or she begins to make sense of the issue; then they move on to something else. What a powerful lesson that offers for Christian leaders—ask why until it begins to make sense and then move on! Why does this organization exist? Why do these people work here day after day? Why have we experienced failure/success? Why are we doing things this way? Why did we purchase that?

Portrait of a Christian Leader

Ask that question about everything. Write down your responses, and patterns will begin to develop. Corporations and organizations across the land have mission statements hanging in an office or on a wall in the lobby that individuals spent time developing. Nevertheless, a careful examination often proves that what is written and what is actually being accomplished are two different things. After reading your mission statement, an outsider should be able to discern who you are and what your mission is all about. If you read your mission statement and it requires someone to stand over your shoulder to explain what it means and how it is meted out in your organization, it is simply not effective.

Christian leaders have the greatest example of mission exemplified in the life of Jesus Christ. Jesus offers hints of His mission throughout the account of His life as recorded in the Gospels. At twelve years old, He asks His parents, "Didn't you know I had to be in my Father's house?" (Luke 2:49). By the Sea of Galilee, He speaks to a few fishermen and offers them a glimpse of what their destiny could be when He says, "Come, follow me ... and I will send you out to fish for people" (Matthew 4:19).

After gaining a following, He presents the reality of His mission in a few words: "Let us go to somewhere else—to the nearby villages—so I can preach there also. That is why I have come" (Mark 1:38). Drawing closer to the end, He speaks more plainly to them, "For the Son of Man came to seek and to save the lost" (Luke 19:10). Finally, on the day He will die, He tells Pilate, "The reason I was born and came into the world is to testify to the truth" (John 18:37). His mission was clear, and the perpetuation of that mission has existed since then.

It matters not whether you lead a small business or a Fortune 500 company, the clarity of organizational mission will keep you and your organization on track. It will enable you to make the right decisions with regards to products, employees, partnerships, and future planning. Those who work for you and work with you should not have to wonder why. The mission should be clear and repeated easily. It should be a memorable statement about the end goal of everything you do.

Every organization starts out with an idea or concept from which to derive the purpose of the organization. More formal organizations may start out with that purpose as a written statement declaring what they hope to accomplish or achieve. Informal organizations may never formalize that purpose in writing; however, it clearly exists in the way the business is conducted. It is this unwritten, often unspoken mode of operation that needs to be developed, definitively stated, and effectively communicated.

If you say that you operate by a statement that hangs in the lobby or in a meeting room of your organization that no one knows about, you have deceived yourself. The mission statement should be alive; it should be the reference for every decision, not a random statement that ends up on the organizational letterhead. If you cannot repeat it right now (without looking) and if your leaders do not know it, then it needs to be revisited. The goal should be to have every person in the organization, from the newest employees to the veterans, be able to say it with conviction. If they do not know it, then they are not making decisions accordingly and cohesion is suffering.

Organizational Structure

Fundamentally, the leader must evaluate whether the organizational structure that is currently in place facilitates or hinders the mission. Ask the question, "Can we do what we say we must do?" This is not easily answered. I encourage you to take some time and evaluate your mission statement in light of this question. It may be a question you need to share with others in the organization. It is not uncommon for a Christian leader to become myopic. He or she becomes so focused on pleasing God in the tasks at hand that it is easy to miss the proverbial forest for the trees. If you spend several days or weeks determining a response to this topic, it will be time well invested.

There is no organizational structure that is better than the next. Each type of structure lends itself to either success or failure depending on the people involved, the product being developed, or the service being offered. Rather than produce a long list of organizational structures that often serve to inhibit creativity, Christian leaders should carefully consider the end goal and take the steps necessary to structure the organization in whatever way is best to accomplish the mission.

Parts of the organization may need to be centralized with a strong leader directing their daily work. Other parts of the organization may thrive in a decentralized structure where individual units are empowered to make decisions on their own, independent of the whole. Both structures may work depending on what needs to be accomplished and the culture of the teams involved.

Portrait of a Christian Leader

Among all the organizational structures found in today's businesses, the team model is most often the choice among Christian leaders. In this model, individual members complement the gifts, experience, and talents of the other members. This is the model touted by the apostle Paul in 1 Corinthians 12. Paul never says that we should build teams for Christian ministry or business, but the idea is birthed here, and it bears some consideration. Paul calls believers gathered in a corporate worship service a body—one unit, where each member contributes according to his or her gifts. The same thing is true in every organization, regardless of if it is acknowledged or not. The company expects them to act corporately to accomplish the mission and individually as it relates to their specific gift or task.

As a Christian leader, I recognize that every member of my organization is gifted in some unique way and the best way to utilize that gift is to develop a team to accomplish the tasks necessary for success. In a similar way, members of a baseball team cannot all play the same positions. They play the positions for which they were trained to win the game. This should be our goal as Christian leaders—to build a team that operates as one unit to win whatever game we are playing.

Communicating/Responding to the Mission

Once we have identified the mission and facilitated the structure to accomplish that mission, our work is still not finished. We get distracted, we get confused, we get sidetracked, and all that happens before breakfast. As I have matured, repetition has become my friend. I tell myself the same thing over and over. I write things down on my planner, my phone, a notepad, and even on my hand, and still I forget! If I forget where I put my to do list when the ink is still wet, I can rest assured that those working with me will also forget why we do what we do. We will focus on getting the job done and forget who we are serving. We will complete the task at hand and fail to realize the long-term implications of our decisions. Just because you cannot remember that last sentence you just read does not mean you throw in the towel. (How many of you just re-read the last sentence?) We must come up with creative ways to help us and those around us remember what we are striving for each day.

Once again, we turn to our role model in order to learn how to keep the mission in the forefront of our organizations. Jesus constantly reminded His disciples that His end goal was to die. He told them repeatedly, and yet, they were surprised when it happened. The mission must be woven into the fabric of everything you do as an organization. It must be communicated so frequently that you start to tire from hearing about it. It is about at that point that others are just starting to get it.

Adherence to the mission and understanding of how each component contributes to the whole is the only way to build a strong organization. If the mission is only seen at board meetings, stated at company functions, or understood by the insiders in the organization, it is not really your team's mission. It should be simple enough to be understood by every person at every level of the organization. No one should ever have to wonder who your organization is or what you are about. The mission should captivate, motivate, and activate those within your organization.

It should be shared with new employees at the onset of employment, and those employees should see it in the way everything in the organization is structured. If new employees do not see it in the way business is conducted, it is likely to not have an impact on the way they perform their jobs. This is too important to be left to chance; intentional communication should produce measurable results.

Response to the mission must be carefully considered and frequently measured. This can be done by asking the question, "If the mission statement were not written down, would it still show up in the way we conduct our daily business?" If the answer is no, then you must process the "Why?" with careful and deliberate action. If the answer is yes, then you are on the right track, but continuing to make an impact is a never-ending journey. If excellence is part of your mission, would your team members perform their jobs with excellence if they were not told? If service is a part of the mission, would your employees be serving without being told? This is real-time testing with real-time results, and the answers will be staring you in the face.

How do your customers respond to the mission? Do they shrug their shoulders and laugh? Do they nod their heads in agreement? Are they telling their friends? Have they become one of your greatest assets for advertising? Response to the mission is internal as well as external. Your employees "doing the mission" means very little if the customers are not "feeling the mission" in the way you perform your work.

If the leaders in every level of your organization must work hard at making it a reality, there is little chance you will be effective. Even on their off days, the employees need to be breathing and walking the mission because customers do not wait for us to be "on." If it is not a natural part of who the organization is, chances are your employees are not responding to the mission you are taking them on. It should be a natural byproduct of who you are and what you do daily.

A great response to your mission statement may not be easy, but it should come as a natural extension of the culture you have created. Exercise discipline to never miss an opportunity to plant the seeds of your mission in the hearts of your employees from the moment they come in the front door. Their first experience may not be at an interview; it may be as a customer. In fact, one of the greatest rewards of an effective mission is to have those you are serving become the ones who are serving in your organization because they believe in what you are doing. Long before the mission is communicated, it is experienced; make sure they are experiencing the right thing.

Increasing Employee Involvement

I am presenting a Christian message in this book, and at its core, the message is simple (the lessons we learn from the life of Jesus always are). Think for a moment of the level of *employee* involvement Jesus gained from those following Him. They were willing to leave everything based on a promise (which was ultimately fulfilled, I might add). They were willing to suffer for it, even though they seldom understood what they had gotten into. They were willing to continue even after the founder was gone. They were willing to give everything they had, fully expending themselves in the process. Eventually, like their example, they were willing to suffer and give their lives to see it perpetuated.

I realize there are those who will find fault with my analogy. They will point to the fact that Jesus was offering eternal life, and re-connection to God was the goal. While our organizations may not even be close to any of that, the analogy still rings true. Do we believe in what we are doing? If yes, it should bear the mark of the Creator because of our involvement. If you do not really believe in what you are doing, stop and find something else you can give your time and your life to. How can we expect our employees to be willing to go the extra mile and give all they have to this cause, if we do not fully believe it is worth the effort? Perhaps this is a new concept for you. Maybe you

Portrait of a Christian Leader

want the employees to work so you will get rich. There is nothing wrong with making a profit, but is the profit solely for your benefit or the benefit of His kingdom?

This is not a popular message, but if we want to increase employee involvement, we must be willing to ask ourselves hard questions that demand even harder answers. This could be the reason you are reading this book. If your employees are putting in their time and giving you a solid week's work, why should they give more? Let them see the results of their labor; let them see that their jobs are making a difference. If the truth is that there is no real impact, go back and reread this chapter. Create a mission statement that honors the one relationship that you will take with you when you pass from this world to the next. If your employees understand the impact they are truly making, you will increase involvement.

Another way to increase employee involvement is to allow them a voice. Let them know their opinions and ideas matter. Give them a voice, a platform from which to express their thoughts—both the good and the not-so-good. Take time to listen to them and do it on purpose. Taking an afternoon to hear their stories, issues, and concerns may result in more productivity for the rest of the month than you ever dreamed. Everyone wants to be heard; they want someone to hear what they have to say—they want to share their story. They want to know that someone will listen to them, so give it a try. Rather than list a number of ways to give your employees a voice, let your imagination run wild with ideas, ask God to show you how, and ask your employees how to help you hear them—it will happen!

Employee participation is largely determined by the level of ownership an employee feels. When they realize their voices are important and their ideas can come to life, nothing will prevent them from being involved in the place where they spend the bulk of their time each week. Without them, you cannot do what you are doing, so let them know it and listen to their dreams. They will be empowered and your leadership will go to another level. Trying this may give birth to the most profitable season yet, and you and your team will have more fun by just giving it a shot.

Try It!

Talk is cheap. You can sit on this and try to avoid it, but I have prayed that as you read this, it will grip your heart and never let it go. I believe that will happen and I believe you will give it a try. In addition, I hope you do not miss this opportunity to be a transformational leader.

1. Pull out your mission statement and ask God if this is what His vision is for your organization. Do not try to do this in one sitting; it may take some time. Many Christian leaders believe they have heard from God and are following Him the best way possible. You may be wrong, and this is one way to discover His plan anew. Write down the things you feel God is saying to you about your organization's mission.

   _____

   _____

   _____

2. Once you feel as if you have connected with God regarding your organizational mission, bring in some of your key leaders and invite them to join you in the journey of re-discovery. Write down the names of several people you may want to include in this journey.

Missional Leader

a. _____

b. _____

c. _____

d. _____

CHAPTER 4 Evidence-Based Leader

Research is Imperative

In order to convince others that our products are better than our competition, we spend money. In fact, most companies pull out all the stops to prove they have exactly what you are looking for. Then, if that was not good enough for our customers, it is commonplace for them to ask countless people what they think about a product before they purchase it. Then, they research it. They check ratings, prices, and comparative reports, and they ask their neighbors and co-workers. They do their homework for virtually everything they buy and use. From toasters and automobiles to recipes and doctors, they want the facts before they decide. Most people seem to bank on the evidence compiled from their families and friends before involving themselves in something that may not be deemed worthy of their time.

Conducting research and polling our families and friends about things we purchase seems to be a normal process, but it seems to break down when we think about addressing problems or spending money in the workplace. The closest many come to researching anything business related is reading a review or asking a veteran employee if that is how it was done before. This is a sad reality for many organizations. Time and money are spent on everything except proving out a strategy before we embark on it. Why does this seem to be the common practice?

At least part of the reason is perpetuation; we do what we have been taught. All of us have been in situations where an action produced a certain reaction. We have files in our minds that are filled with these scenarios. As a result, we are less likely to try new things or even re-try old things because we think we *know* what will happen. The reality is we often do not know if the results will be the same because there are so many variables involved.

Evidence-based management is all about making decisions based on evidence, not just experience. Experience is a tough teacher—relentless and harsh—and not always the best teacher. If through our experiences, we make the right decisions, then experience has been a great teacher.

However, if we learn the wrong lessons or, from that, develop the wrong habits, then our experience may have hurt our future decisions. Making decisions based on facts as opposed to experiences is hard work and can be time-consuming, but it is worth it in the long run.

Leaders who attempt to implement an evidence-based system need to be prepared for roadblocks. This is not the standard mode of operation for most companies, as decisions are usually made at one level and implemented on another level. Trial and error, experience, longevity, and a hundred other reasons offer a foundation to *not* use evidence-based management. Taking the time to work through perceived and real challenges is seldom fun or popular; consequently, the path of least resistance tends to lead us back to "the way we have always done it!"

As Christian leaders, we should be unconventional—willing to launch ourselves and our organizations on the path less traveled. That is the example of Jesus. He did not come as a warrior king or a political hero; He came as a servant and died the death of a sinner to reconcile humanity to God. We must follow His lead to chart the course and set the pace to do things differently.

No More Assumptions

There is no way to measure the money, time, or potential lost in assumptions. If we are blessed enough to have limitless reserves of time and money, then assumptions could be the norm in our organizations. As no leader would say that about his or her organization, perhaps we should consider the concept of evidence-based management. When factoring budgets, most leaders consider the "what if..." factor. Doing so compels us to gather reserves just in case something happens. While there will always be those unexpected occurrences, why not take some of the reserves in your budget and invest in tomorrow today with evidence-based management?

So, what are the strategies we can use to incorporate evidence-based decision-making into our leadership inventory? Develop a team comprised of members from different departments and task this collaborative effort to think, plan, and research a problem thoroughly. Invest your energy, time, and money in that collaboration and watch what happens. Evidence-based management allows teams to explore thinking outside of the traditional organizational structures and boxes. If departments only work within themselves, they become introverted, which can eventually cause an implosion. The evidence-based team approach encourages non-traditional thinking. It challenges norms and proves the process rather than just assuming the process is correct.

We live in a fast-paced global environment. Packages travel across the world overnight and the small manufacturing plant in Hometown, USA, is buying and selling goods internationally. Assuming you have the answer, assuming you understand the problem, assuming your company *go-to* guy or gal will always have the right answer for every situation is elementary thinking. Invest the time today to prove out your theories to avoid wasting precious assets tomorrow.

This is not the quick fix that most organizational leaders are looking for. (You know the type—perhaps it is you.) They need an answer now and would rather take their chances with a guess than invest in discovery. They would rather try something three times instead of just working through the tough questions up front. You know, they "need to keep things going," "to stop moving forward is moving backward," and "as long as we are doing something, nothing is wasted; it is an investment." Whether you practice evidence-based management or not, you are making an investment. The investment comes on the front end when you research or the back end as you regroup to try a different approach.

The healthcare industry leads the way in evidence-based management. We would not dream of participating in a study or treatment based on the hunch of one doctor. If a neurosurgeon had a theory that he or she could perform a surgery with an unproven technique and needed a human to test it, few of us would sign up. In fact, when facing a major surgery or procedure, the surgeon will often quote statistics to you in order to build your confidence. "You have a ninety percent chance of coming through this with few complications." Based on that proven statistic, you make a decision that may forever alter the way you live your life. Imagine going through the surgery prep and before you are sedated, the surgeon tells you, "I got those statistics from my friend Joe who runs a restaurant down the street. He has a few friends who have gone through this procedure and let me know you would probably be okay!" Obviously, this is not a comforting scenario. The reality is that is how many of today's organizations operate.

A manager has a hunch or talks with other managers and begins to make slight adjustments to alter the outcomes in your organization. Perhaps a member of management goes to a conference and brings back a new idea that is immediately implemented based on the proven success this change had in another company, in another town, in another market, "but it should work for us too." Sounds silly, right? Even still, I would imagine most of us can point to at least one organizational change we have endured based on this same faulty logic.

Few people have the luxury of just trying things for the fun of it. Leaders should start with a sense of urgency and recognize time is not a commodity we can afford to waste. You can start by taking the time to implement this strategy in small ways. Decide that you will stop making decisions based on assumptions, faulty logic, and popular opinion. Decide that regardless of what your organization does, you will invest the time, energy, and resources to base your decisions on evidence whenever it is feasibly possible.

Taking Time—Now or Later

By this point, some of you probably recognize the value of thoroughly exploring situations and options before making decisions, but you do not know where to begin. Perhaps there is no data for the decisions with which you are faced. In those cases, a collaborative team could prove to be invaluable. Taking the time to work through the hard questions and limited options of a situation may seem like an exercise in futility, but investing in the process is always worth the effort. Those who choose to practice evidence-based management understand the investment is best spent at the beginning of the project rather than at the end.

Even if the actual profit analysis of the project turns out to break even, evidence-based management still helps. Investing in the front end of a project will involve more people in the process. The initial investment process serves to enhance your team by building team unity. The outcome is not the work of one man or woman but of the collaborative effort of the team. As the members of this team return to their respective departments, they carry the realization of that collaboration back with them. Everyone wins!

Promote the value of collaboration and watch how your organization begins to gel. Let the people you employ see your dependence on them and they will always respond. Let's face it: research and exploration are not always fun. It takes time and it requires a huge investment, but the results are often worth the wait.

Evidence-Based Leader

To make this work, you must be willing to stay the course and not skip the process. The easiest thing to do would be to take a quick path of least resistance, that is, to fall back into the patterns you have been accustomed to and let the naysayers convince you to do what "everyone else is doing!" You must be fully convinced of this personally or your subordinates will immediately begin to recognize your uncertainty. The natural response is to operate in a manner they are accustomed to following—don't do it!

I urge you to practice evidence-based leadership and be determined to make it a standard practice in your organization. It will attract innovators, and they will think outside the traditional corporate boxes. Your followers will see you as a leader and not easily swayed by popular opinion, and soon they may be investing in their own research initiatives. Cultural shift in any organization is not easy work, but if you are willing to go against the grain and try something new, you will notice an organizational shift that is worth the investment on the front end.

Try It!

1. Begin your journey to evidence-based leadership by spending some time thinking about an area of your

organization where you want to start this process. Some of you have already thought of areas where you could implement this strategy, while others will have to think and pray and wait for God to reveal this answer. Write down the areas, projects, and departments where evidence-based decision-making should be practiced first.

_____

_____

_____

_____

2. Critically consider the people and areas of business where the greatest resistance will come from and write them here. Knowing where these pitfalls may lie will give you opportunity to strategize before you begin.

_____

_____

_____

CHAPTER 5 Team Leader

Organizational Fit

How can leaders know if a potential new employee will fit in? How can we determine if this person will become an asset or a liability? I wish I knew how to answer those questions definitively, but I do not. I do know that when trying to determine whether a new candidate is the right man or woman for the job, it is common to look at everything except organizational fit. People come and fill out applications, and we weed through them looking at experience, credentials, and accomplishments. Based largely on those areas, we decide whether to invite that person back for an interview. Should we consider more than that before making that call? The answer to that is a resounding yes!

I believe it is possible to screen resumes, applications, and all the other particulars that come with them through the eyes of organizational fit. From the beginning of the process until a new person is filling out a W-4, we should be considering how this candidate fits within the culture of our organization. This brings up the first point of concern in this process—before we can hire people to fill our vacancies, we must know who we are. What is the culture of your organization?

Determine the norms and counter-norms of your organization. What are the commonalities among the different departments and leaders? Do the people there know the names of one another's spouses and children? Do they only interact while performing their jobs? The list could go on and on. The point here is not to present an exhaustive list, but to get you thinking about the culture, the environment, and the atmosphere. I once worked in a job where everyone was all about their work. There was very little interaction, no joking, and no laughter. I lasted about three weeks. I was miserable, and I think I made most of my co-workers uneasy. I could do the job, they liked my work, and job security was not an issue. Nevertheless, I was dying a little more and more each day. I did not fit the culture of that organization, and it was apparent to all of us.

The job that followed this one was very different. People hung out together all the time outside of work. We were always playing simple, innocent jokes on one another. We laughed all the time. I fit like a glove and stayed there for a while. The point is simple: spend time up front to ensure the individual fits or spend more time hiring a replacement when he or she leaves. Either way, you will spend time and money, but one allows you to skip a lot of aggravation for everyone involved.

Taking the time to understand organization fit will compel you to find the right person, not just someone to get the job done. I want my employees to thrive. I want them looking forward to coming to work. I want them to give more than I could possibly pay them for. If those are going to be the characteristics of my organization, it will require work—hard work—and I expect it to pay off in both the short and long terms. Doing so will benefit everyone, and it will show in every aspect of your business.

As Christian leaders, we are reminded that we do not all fill the same function (see Romans 12:4-8); each of us is gifted uniquely by our Creator. Like pieces of a giant puzzle, we fit together to create a picture. If all of my employees are corner pieces, our puzzle will be incomplete. As a Christian leader, you should expend every effort to ensure your employees do not just fit, but that they are the right piece of your organizational puzzle to complete the picture.

Job Fit

A Christian leader recognizes the uniqueness of each follower. All of us can fill a slot and accomplish things we are not specifically gifted at. However, a Christian leader should strive to find that individual who best fits that empty slot. When we find that sweet spot we were uniquely crafted by our heavenly Father to fill, we operate at our optimum and so do our organizations. Christian leaders who recognize that also understand how that affects the overall organizational structure.

Placing people in positions they are not uniquely gifted for puts a strain on them and on those around them. They may accomplish the task and sometimes even do it very well; nevertheless, the pressure that comes from trying to fit in is not comfortable at all. (It is like trying to put on

Team Leader

those jeans that were worn five to ten years ago—it may be possible but not comfortable.) Paul describes it this way, "Now to each one the manifestation of the Spirit is given for the common good ... and he distributes them to each one, just as he determines" (1 Corinthians 12:7, 11). Considering how individuals fit in an organization serves to build a well-rounded and high-functioning team.

While many things affect the overall motivation of an individual, being in the wrong job has to be among the biggest. It can show up in many ways, but one of the more obvious ways is in employee motivation. The lack of motivation is not the sole indicator of a job fit issue, but it will often be among the ones most easily identified. Most of us can accomplish a number of things out of sheer will and determination, but doing so as a regular part of our activity will lead to burnout.

A typical scenario may look like this: Someone has the right qualifications and skill sets to perform a job. This person operating in his or her area of strength will often excel in this position. The leaders making personnel decisions see a competent leader and a proven success record, and they determine that the best way to serve the individual and the organization is to promote that person to the next level within the organization. So, with a new title, a new salary, and dreams bigger than he or she can contain, the employee enters the next level and enters the all-too-common realm of repeated failure. No one can understand why the poster child for success has suddenly become an example for failure. Success at one level does not guarantee success at the next level, but that is the way many organizations promote people.

The person working in this capacity—outside the realm of his or her expertise—will begin to have less and less of an impact in the organization. As that happens, personal motivation begins to wane, and that begins to affect the morale of the department in which they work. At this point, it would be common for most organizations to focus solely on the individual rather than consider how he or she fits within the culture of their current job. One of the first things they consider is whether this person is the best fit for the organization (should we let him or her go?). I have seen it happen, and if you have been in business for any length of time, you have likely seen it too. Generally, the person in question begins to experience frustration and burnout as he or she works beyond his or her own giftings; the job they have been asked to fill is not a good fit for them, and few people have the ability to recognize it.

Upon evaluating motivation issues of employees, in his book *Organization Change,* Warner Burke encourages us to consider the following three areas: task requirements, individual skills/abilities, and individual needs/values.[2] Considering this, ask yourself the following questions:

1. What are the primary tasks required for this position?

2. What are the primary skills/abilities this person possesses?

3. From what I know about this person, is there anything about this position that conflicts with his or her values?

4. From what I know about this person, will this position fit the needs he or she requires to be effective long-term?

Taking the time to evaluate the position and the person in question may alleviate a lot of tension and aggravation in the long run. When you see the individual experiencing undue stress, lack of motivation, and overall dissatisfaction, as the leader, you should always consider the conditions that may have changed this person from the success he or she was to the struggling person that is now in front of you. A Christian leader should always evaluate his or her employees in light of both internal and external conditions. If a person no longer seems to fit in your organization, it could be that he or she is trying to fit into a role God has not designed them for.

I once worked with an older civilian employee when I served in the United States Air Force. I remember asking him one time why he was content to do the manual labor I was required to do as opposed to striving for a management position somewhere. His answer was so simple and so profound I have never forgotten it. He said, "I was not made for that type of work. I am a good machinist and would not make a very good paper pusher." When it comes to understanding job fit, this man understood what he was talking about.

Diagnosing Problems and Motivational Issues

I have already noted that job fit is one common problem and motivational issue often overlooked in our organizations, but how can you train yourself to look beyond the surface to understand the root problem? It takes time, patience, and lots of practice. Many people can tell you if they are happy, sad, or mad, but fewer can tell you why and even fewer than that can tell you why with accuracy. Most organizations are operating at such breakneck speeds, they are content to put a bandage on a compound fracture and keep moving. Taking a cough drop for a sore throat and cough syrup for a deep cough may alleviate some of your symptoms, but if you have pneumonia, they will not bring long-term relief.

I am a firm believer in the reality that one leader cannot see all the existing or potential problems of an organization or a department of that organization. As such, I suggest you develop a problem-solving team (PST) for your organization. A PST should consist of at least one individual from at least four different departments to not exceed seven people (a consideration derived from George Miller's essay, "The Magical Number Seven," as quoted by Malcolm Gladwell).[3] A PST should be granted access to behind-the-scenes data and allowed the opportunity to critically analyze issues and potential problem areas in every department. Rather than relying on the expertise of one individual, you will be leaning on the collective insight of this group to diagnose problems. You may not be able to hire a consultant to come in and evaluate every area in your organization, but by sparing some time and allowing extreme latitude with your PST, you are developing a team of internal experts.

This team will not supplant your leaders' ability to diagnose problems, but it does create buy-in and ownership among the various departments as it relates to problem-solving. Diagnosing problems and motivational issues is not something easily taught in a three- or four-step process. It will require an investment of your time and your patience. You will miss problems in the beginning, but as you learn what to look for and how to utilize your PST to the organization's full advantage, problems will become easier to recognize, easier to diagnose, and easier to overcome.

How do our most valued assets lose their motivation? Why do employees have periods of time where they seem to "check out"? Once again, the reasons are varied, and an exhaustive list is impossible to create. These questions are closely related to the one we just examined. Often motivation has taken a vacation because a problem exists. The problem seldom rests on one individual or one department. It may show up in one person or department first, and once it does, the tipping point is fast approaching. So, what can be done to avoid the problem?

First, as Christian leaders, we should always look to Christ as our example. Jesus knew His disciples; those men who would carry His message to the ends of the earth had names, families, histories, and futures. Jesus knew where each one fit, what they would do, and who they were best suited to reach. My guess is the same could not be said of most leaders today. The people who work for our causes are more than just a name, a product, or a profit margin. They have dreams, expectations, and hopes. I found that one of the greatest gifts a leader can give an employee is the opportunity to be heard.

Everyone has a story. Few things serve to enhance motivation more than taking the time to listen to your people. Let them tell you about their dreams and ideas. Let them tell you how they feel without retaliating. Listen to the story of that receptionist or that person in housekeeping. They are just as important to the flow of information and control of the rumor mill as your managers and department leaders. Listening to that person will certainly not solve all your motivation issues, but it is a simple place to start. The people who work for you are not just the way you generate profit; they are human beings created by God for

Portrait of a Christian Leader

His glory. They may never know that unless you allow them the opportunity to feel as if their story matters too.

Motivational issues often begin when people feel like their opinion does not matter or that they are working for an organization as opposed to a person. They should not act differently when you are around. They should not become anxious or nervous because you are there. Your presence as a leader should bring them comfort and confidence. You know them, they know you; you are all working on the same team, and there is connection, not fragmentation.

Motivation rises and falls on leadership. If your people are not motivated, do not blame them. First, look at your leadership. Are you providing the encouragement, the stability, and the leadership they need to excel? If you can only find fault without accepting some of the responsibility for this condition in your organization, you may be the problem. You can hide behind blame and finger-pointing for a while, but it will eventually surface. When the PST diagnoses your leadership or lack of leadership as a problem, you will be forced to take responsibility based on their direction, and that can be a most humbling experience.

Developing a Measurable Leader/Follower Plan

Measurable plans often cause those in leadership to squirm a bit. Measurable plans require accountability, and while we may want to hold others accountable, we seldom feel as strongly about it when it comes to us as leaders. I cannot lead if I am not effective, and I am seldom in the best position to measure my own effectiveness. A measurable plan requires the involvement of those around us to ensure an unbiased measurement is being taken.

As I consider my leadership and how it relates to my subordinates today, I like to think I am doing well. I can point to their positive attitudes while at work and how dedicated they are to each other and their tasks. I would point out their willingness to work beyond their requirements and sacrificially give to one another. In my own evaluation as their leader, I see all the things I want to see. I see all the things that make me look good, that give the appearance that I know what I am doing. But if I really want an accurate picture, if I want a measurable plan, I must allow my employees to speak for themselves. When I speak for them, I would seldom critique myself negatively. However, the truth is realized when they speak for themselves.

A measurable plan includes goal setting, date setting, and forecasting. I cannot measure my performance against perceived numbers or idealized goals I have created in my head. I write things down and ask those above and below me to keep me accountable for the things I say I will do. This requires time for evaluation from those I answer to and from those who answer to me. As a leader, it may be a common part of my job description to set goals and work toward them. However, if you really want to see what you are capable of, share your goals with your employees and watch how they will hold you accountable.

If I set goals for my team, meet with them regularly to evaluate where we are in the process, and offer counsel on how to achieve the goals, we should expect some progress. The same thing is true when developing a measurable leader plan. I can set all sorts of lofty goals that sound great and aspire to nothing. However, if I know my progress is going to be monitored on a regular basis, I am much more likely to set realistic goals and work toward them systematically.

I cannot begin to tell of all the leaders I have coached, sat under, and listened to who wanted to excel at their jobs. The same leaders who will pay to attend a conference in order to learn how to increase the organization's profit margin will often wince when told the most effective way to reach your personal goals is to ask your subordinates to hold you accountable. When I have encouraged them to set personal goals and tell their subordinates, they have thought I was crazy. Nevertheless, the ones who have done it usually marvel at the progress they make in a short time.

The key to a measurable plan is accountability. You can build accountability into your plan through a variety of means, and while I have touted the implications of utilizing your subordinates, that is certainly not the only way to develop a measurable plan. A measurable plan must be written down. It must include dates and benchmarks whereby you can judge progress and performance to adjust.

Lastly, my personal preference is to publish the plan in a place where others can see it on a regular basis. There is nothing like letting people know what you expect of them and what they can expect of you to increase productivity. If this process concerns you, try it with something small first and watch the reaction. You will be amazed at the response, and your employees will be amazed you are doing it. Once you model a measurable plan for yourself, it will be easier to set goals for your employees. When it is recognized that everyone is measured in the same way, things will change at every level.

Try It!

I realize this is not an easy step, but reading about it and passing judgment is taking the easy way out. I am confident it will be worth the risk.

1. When considering the culture of your organization, you need to recognize those nonnegotiable areas that identify who your company is. Identify five characteristics of the culture of your organization (consider things that are nonnegotiable for you).

    a. _____

    b. _____

    c. _____

    d. _____

    e. _____

f. _____

2. Can you identify any other areas that currently define your organizational culture that you are not satisfied with? If so, write it down and share why it may need to change.

_____
_____
_____
_____

CHAPTER 6 Communicating Leader

Effective communication should be one of the hallmarks of every Christian leader. If we have not achieved some mastery of it, we should apply all we are—every faculty of our being—to becoming adept at communication. By His words, God created. In fact, as the Bible begins, we find a formless earth, empty and dark, and then He spoke and nothing was the same (see Genesis 1:1-5). Countless Christian leaders find themselves in organizational chaos—at a loss for how to address the issues at hand—and until they learn to communicate, they will always be at a loss. Consequently, learning how to be an effective communicator should be a top priority.

It is worth mentioning that I have intentionally decided not to separate communication from listening because effective communication always includes listening, or it is simply not effective. It takes two people actively listening and responding to one another to have effective communication. That type of communication can happen face to face, over the phone, through a text, or by the written word. In fact, if you are reading this and responding to the sections at the end of each chapter, this is effective communication. With it, organizations thrive and are vibrant; without it, they are lifeless and dying.

Evaluating Communication Styles

Every leader has practiced a variety of communication styles and approaches all of their lives. We speak to young children differently than we do our peers or even our parents. Our styles, words, and even voice inflection change as the situations of our lives dictate. We must create, develop, or agree upon a common ground if effective communication is going to take place.

I have worked in many different settings where the ages of the workforce have spanned decades. The level of expertise of the workers as well as their geographic origin always had a tremendous impact on how communication took place. This *workforce* is not unlike our own families; family members respond to things differently, and over time, we learn to anticipate how each of them will react in different situations. Any parent with more than one child understands this concept perfectly.

My purpose in writing this chapter is not to evaluate and offer a critique on the myriad ways to communicate. I simply want the Christian leader to carefully consider how he or she is modeling Christ in speech and communication. In my opinion, there are four common communication styles that leaders practice.

We talk. Every leader has been on the giving and receiving end of this type of communication. This is where a leader has an idea and talks about it incessantly. It shows up in every form of communication, every conversation, and every action, but all it is is talk. There is no plan, no rhyme or reason to the conversation; in fact, all it does is consume oxygen. It is not uncommon for both leaders and followers to get frustrated by this type of communication. Like the proverbial broken record of old (I know I just dated myself), it is the same thing over and over, without any real purpose.

With all that is in you as a leader, refrain from this kind of communication. Be careful to not become infatuated by the sound of your own voice. To do so will cause your greatest assets to resign the organization, leaving only your greatest liabilities. People of action, with a sense of purpose and ambition, will seldom stay any place where talk dominates and action is an anomaly. You know you have fallen victim to this type of communication if those around you often have no response to your words. In this instance, your talk, your message, your communication has become so empty that growth has stopped, innovation has disappeared, and, organizationally speaking, you are one step away from being extinct.

This type of communication is dangerous, stifling, and all too common in organizations. If we are to be modeling Christ to our employees, the last thing those employees need is to hear us rambling—without purpose or objective. Every Christian leader owes it to his or her organization and to Jesus Christ to surround themselves with people who will never settle for this type of ineffectiveness. While it may cause you to feel threatened at times, one of the greatest assets a Christian leader can have is men and women who will question them in private, challenge them in the meeting room, and follow them with unfaltering loyalty in the organization at large once a consensus has been reached.

We talk at them. Another term I like to use for this type of communication is the drill sergeant model. When I was in basic training, there was no discussion, no dialogue. The training instructor barked out an order and we blindly followed. The message was received and obeyed, but there was no relationship. The only requirement to talk at someone is that they are breathing. They do not have to know you, like you, or even listen to you; they simply need to do and that is enough. While this type of communication may work for basic training, it is not that effective in the workplace.

It takes no buy-in, intuition, or insight to speak at someone, and that makes it a very common occurrence. Talking at someone allows a leader to simply say, "Well, I told them how to do it and they would not listen; it is not my fault." In other words, it enables you to pass the proverbial buck. Sad as it is, when a leader reaches this point, massive intervention needs to occur but seldom does. Talking at someone typically frustrates the sender and the receiver because little happens.

We talk to them. The primary difference in this form of communication from the two previously mentioned is this one requires relationship. If I am talking to an individual, I must be aware of his or her reception of the message I am sending. I watch their reactions, respond to their body language, and even grant them an opportunity for response from time to time. Talking to someone requires more than just disseminating a message; it requires engagement. In addition, this also requires me to make adjustments in the way I communicate in order to gain maximum buy-in from the receiver.

The responsibility of representing Christ to those around me is among my most important tasks as a Christian leader. I cannot abuse the faith of my team by ignoring them; I must recognize it is part of my duty to nurture their faith. I accomplish this by talking *to* my team. Teaching them to get the message (whether personal or organizational) is crucial, and I want them to see Him through the process. Talking to them requires both parties to be fully engaged in the process, sending the message, receiving the message, and responding to the message.

Christian leaders must model that the importance of sending the message is equally as important as receiving and responding to the message. I never want my team to simply *do* what I am communicating to them: I need them to hear my heart, read my intent, and respond in a way that I know they are willing to go above and beyond the call. Successful communication is not only achieved by a message well-delivered but also by a message well-received. Christian leaders must accept responsibility for both the delivery and the reception, by knowing and caring about our employees. If your followers know you and you know them, talking *to* them will be a normal activity.

We talk with them. I consider this the strongest and most meaningful form of communication possible in an organization. It includes sending and receiving the message along multiple layers and levels. Whereas other types of communication focus primarily on the sender giving the message and the receiver processing the message, this type of communication requires both parties to act as sender and receiver throughout the dialogue. Having both parties enmeshed in the communication process is where we are more likely to achieve maximum communication.

Much of what we call communication is simply one party waiting for the other to stop talking so he or she can begin talking. Consequently, there are a lot of words flowing between individuals, but little in the way of meaningful conversation. Talking *with* someone requires both parties to listen, to participate, and to respond to what is being communicated. When I talk with my team and they actively listen, and when I listen and they feel empowered to contribute to the conversation, both of us walk away with a greater sense of understanding and accomplishment. Talking with someone implies there is mutual contribution to the dialogue.

In organizations where senior leadership has mastered this level of conversation, everyone feels empowered. There is a greater sense of team and connectedness. If I go to my leader and I know that he or she is willing to speak with me, I am much more inclined to open up, think through my responses, and process the consequences of my words. When I realize that my ideas, my contributions, and my challenges will be met with engagement by my superiors, I feel valued. Valued employees are productive employees.

Knowing What Your Team Wants and Needs

Everyone has a story, and that story is about their lives, their experiences, their dreams, and their failures. Make no mistake: your employees, your customers, and your peers want you to know their story. At the core level, every team member wants to know that what he or she brings to the table is valued and appreciated. They want to know that their story matters, and they want you to know their story. How many stories have you allowed your employees to tell you?

Without team players, an organization is empty, lifeless, and unproductive—it simply cannot exist. As a Christian leader, you owe it to your organization, your employees, and God to figure out what your team wants and needs and then exhaust yourself in meeting those wants and needs (of course, common sense should prevail here as well).

I realize that may seem like the leaders become subservient to the followers, and in some regards, that may be necessary. Even if I cannot meet all the desires and needs of my employees, I need to know what they are. To know those things implies relationship; it implies understanding. If there is no place for open, honest interaction between leaders and followers, you may never know their hearts. If you are going to know what their needs and wants are, you are going to have to know them. The key to this element of leadership is relationship.

I have often heard it said that leaders can get too close to those in their organizations. Some would say that to do so will erode the lines between leadership and followership. Without that relationship, the lines between leadership and followership have already eroded. Building relationships with my teams strengthens my leadership credibility and brings an authenticity that has long been void in organizations. I am a real person, a real leader, with real problems, challenges, and questions. My employees do not need to know all of those issues in my life, but allowing them to see my issues takes our relationship to a different level. Then, they may feel comfortable sharing their story.

In their book entitled *The Leadership Challenge,* James Kouzes and Barry Posner report on a study conducted years ago on what employees want in their leaders. Team members reported that the leaders who were most desirable were honest, forward thinking, inspiring, and competent. [4] Every one of these qualities are most noted and appreciated through relationship. Relationship with subordinates does not have to mean being overly touchy-feely or even hanging out together outside of work. However, it does mean that they know us, and we know them. It also means that communication—effective and authentic communication—flows freely both ways.

There will always be things that leaders cannot give their followers, but as the relationship becomes increasingly authentic, both parties understand the value of only asking for things that the other can provide. Once while serving in a small manufacturing facility, management realized that unless paychecks were cut drastically for a time, some people would lose their jobs altogether. There was not one person who was excited about the possibility of a pay cut, but we pulled together and made it through the lean season together. The workforce took a ten percent cut in pay, while the management braced for a twenty-five percent cut for at least the next three months. Not one person was lost during that period, and I attribute that largely to the leadership's willingness to lead the way and be authentic through it all. When the leaders shared the concept, it was done out of relationship, and everyone had come to trust that the ones who signed their paychecks could be trusted to get us all out of this rut. Consequently, the pay cut only lasted one month. Revenues returned, back pay was granted, and together we moved forward.

On the other side, I was a part of another organization where the senior leadership elected to allow the organization to fall into arrears for months. Foreclosure loomed, while the leadership continually passed the buck and would not accept responsibility. The senior leadership team split, and the organization all but dissolved. Many of those in the trenches of this group elected to leave, and chaos ensued.

Employees want leaders who will lead and serve through the adversities and the successes of organizational life. They want leaders who will be authentic when it is easy and when it is difficult. They want to know that they matter—whether that is having someone listen to their stories or granting them an opportunity to be a part of the solution to the company's problems, they want to be more than a production number, more than a warm body performing a mediocre task. They want to matter, and the organizations that learn how to accomplish that will see loyalty that cannot be bought. That type of loyalty is only possible through relationship. Your employees really do matter; make sure they know it!

Analyzing Organizational Conflict

We all know what causes conflict. Conflict happens when *you* fail to fall in step with what *I* have said. Of course, conflict is much more than that, but all too often this is how it is translated: I did not get my way and now we have a problem. Organizational conflict should never be reduced to you against me. Organizational conflict is much bigger than that.

The tendency is to use conflict to attack the symptoms and ignore the root cause. Symptoms are easy to identify, easy to diagnose, and often easily remedied. The problem goes away for a while, but eventually it shows up again and the cycle is repeated. There have been many leaders who have established their credibility on being able to navigate the waters of organizational conflict. The fact that the conflict continues to resurface is sometimes considered job security by those leaders.

In order to adequately analyze organizational conflict, leaders must be willing to look beyond the way it manifests itself. Examining root causes in organizational conflict is not an easy task. It often requires the involvement of several people internally or one person externally. The reason to include others is that if I am analyzing the problem and I am the problem, I may never see it. Christian leaders need to understand that while organizational conflict is normal, it cannot go unchecked. Pretending it does not exist or recognizing it does exist and never doing anything about it is organizational neglect.

I know very few leaders who can analyze organizational conflict objectively. They tend to lean to one side or the other based on personal interests. While larger organizations have the resources to bring consultants from the outside in for evaluation purposes, smaller organizations usually look to their leaders for direction. That option is better than not doing anything, but I would like to suggest a collaborative approach. Begin by identifying five to seven people from different departments who are willing to participate in a conflict resolution team. Depending on the size of your organization, five to seven people may not be feasible. Choose whatever smaller number is best for your situation and move forward.

By drawing people from different departments, with different experiences, talents, and insights, the group is more willing to explore a broader set of outcomes, diagnoses, and remedies. The organization's leader may coordinate this team, but he or she should not be a part of their discussions because he or she tends to illicit a typical response from people, and that is what we want to avoid.

A team that periodically comes together for the purposes of handling conflict keeps the finger-pointing to a minimum and serves to identify trigger points (root causes) in ways that one person cannot do alone. Developing a team internally also promotes a greater sense of accountability throughout the organization. If there is tension among different departments and an outside consultant starts putting the blame on one of them, there is a greater tendency for the other departments to blame them as well. However, if a member of the offending department is a part of a collaborative team, the finger-pointing is kept to a minimum. We are in this together, and until our focus becomes centered on getting through this together, we will stay fixated on finger pointing and playing the blame game.

Try It!

1. I identified four different communication styles at the beginning of this chapter. No one else will ever see this record of your vulnerability, so be honest with yourself. What was the most common type of communication you experienced growing up, and how do you think that has affected your communication style today?

   _____

   _____

Portrait of a Christian Leader

_____

_____

2. As a leader, which communication style would your subordinates say you practice the most? Is this the way you want to be seen? Why or why not?

_____

_____

_____

_____

CHAPTER 7 Change Leader

Change is a good thing for organizations. Competent leaders understand that change is a natural part of organizational life. The competition is changing, the customers are changing, and the organizational culture is constantly changing. Organizations that are not fluid, flowing, and alive quickly become stagnant. They attract substandard people—employees and customers. The competent Christian leader understands this and should strive to be the primary change agent in his or her organization.

Far too many leaders have become highly proficient at being reactive rather than proactive. You know how this works: something happens, and we react. Unfortunately, when we operate this way and become experts at reacting, we find our competition has often beaten us to the punch. Striving to be proactive causes us to think ahead in order

Portrait of a Christian Leader

to prepare for the coming changes. We can do that because we are creating the change. Reactive leaders are those who often over-analyze what has happened. In doing so, they miss what is happening or what is about to happen. Proactive leaders are always looking forward. That is not to say it is unimportant to understand what has happened, but too much focus on the past causes us to become immobile or even move backward.

I know there are some naysayers out there who would argue that only *good* change is good for organizations. Of course, good change is what we should long for; however, even bad change can produce positive results. Change always creates movement, and once the organization begins to move again, things will happen. It's like this: even when less than desirable things happen in our personal lives or in the life of our organization, we are compelled to respond. Even the slightest response or movement can enable us to see organizational life from a different perspective. There have been countless times in my life when I have been compelled to move when I did not want to, only to have that movement result in something positive.

Revolutionary and Evolutionary Change

These two types of change characterize the opposite ends of the spectrum for organizational change. Revolutionary change is exactly what it sounds like—a revolution. It is different, radical, and innovative—it is unlike any change you have experienced. Thoughts of revolutionary change may invoke scenes of the years leading up to 1776. A few revolutionaries sought to build a better country, a better life than they had previously experienced. They were rebels; they fought against the status quo of their day. They dreamed against all odds that they had an answer for what this would-be country needed. Had they listened to their fears, the dissenting voices of some of their leaders, or the norms of the day, who knows where we would all be today?

Christian leaders need to recognize that revolutionary change is exactly what their organization needs from time to time. Stuck in a rut for so long, we either succumb to the expectations of those around us or we can use that rut as a launch pad for a revolution. That is seldom easy, and often those around us feel the need to "correct us" and "get us back on track" into the rut. However, a revolutionary

Christian leader needs to learn how to follow the guidance of the Holy Spirit and march to His beat alone.

Jesus heralded revolutionary change. He introduced His revolutionary ideals with some of His first public words. In Matthew 4:17, He began to preach repentance for the "... kingdom of heaven has come near." This kingdom is unlike any other kingdom known to humanity. It is a place where revolutionary concepts are encouraged and expected. This kingdom of opposites is where we turn the other cheek, go the second mile, and give freely of the things we possess (Matthew 5:38-42). He could have entered the realm of humanity and followed the prescribed course expected of Him, but that would not have fit His revolutionary mindset. He was radical, He was different, and He was a leader of revolutionary change.

Those who follow Him today should strive to look like Him. Whether we lead Fortune 500 companies, work in a local hardware store, lead a Christian ministry, or are still trying to figure out what we want to be when we grow up, we should embrace, encourage, and embody revolutionary change. The creative strength of the Godhead is found in the Holy Spirit, and as He resides in each of us at the point of salvation, there is no reason why we should not be hotbeds of innovative change in whatever industry we find ourselves in.

If you have never asked God for this type of revolutionary change to be a hallmark of your life, stop right now and do it. Ask for the creativity of the Holy Spirit to be manifested in your leadership. This is not wild, destructive change for the sake of change. This is a radical change with purpose and power. Anyone can initiate change in their organization, but revolutionary change inspired by the Holy Spirit will result in promise, hope, and inspiration. It should be a part of every Christian leader's life. Your organization will benefit greatly from your willingness to follow the model of Jesus Christ and be a revolutionary change agent.

While being revolutionary is wild and exciting at times, it is not feasible to think that an organization could or should operate in a revolutionary mind-set all the time. Evolutionary change is the type of change that leaders should be fostering day by day. This type of change looks just like the name it bears—slow, subtle changes over an extended period. It is seldom exciting or exhilarating, but it is always necessary for the health of the organization. We should recognize that change is going to happen whether we foster it or not. Understanding that and carefully planning and executing an evolutionary change process in your organization will enable you to make informed decisions with regards to how change will take place.

Evolutionary changes are always taking place in the life of your organization. People change, products change, and needs change; consequently, the competent, well-informed Christian leader will do well to constantly plan and initiate the evolutionary changes necessary for healthy growth. This requires forethought, strategic planning, and collaboration, and because it requires more work to be an evolutionary change agent, many leaders choose to do nothing beforehand and only react to what is happening. As a result, many opportunities are missed, and your organization suffers the consequences.

Planning for evolutionary change requires diligence and perseverance—this change takes time. Sometimes the changes span a season or the tenure of a poor executive leader, and there are times when the changes you initiate outlast your time in the organization. We do not live in a world that appreciates the delayed gratification of slow evolutionary change. We want it now! We need to see progress last week, and the thought of making this kind of investment in an objective is overwhelming. Nevertheless, all of us can identify changes in our organizations that would be best as a slow, methodical evolutionary process versus the radical shift of revolutionary change.

In order to bring God into our organizations, we need to plan for positive, strategic, Spirit-led change. To simply roll along without a plan is not leading at all. If identifying and processing change is not among your strengths or experience, invest in others who can help your organization cast the vision for necessary change and then empower them to make it happen. Do not delay; get started today!

With measurable goals, it becomes easy to identify the success or failure as the process unfolds. Benchmarks help organizational leaders identify if the means are leading to the desired end. Determining success or failure should happen throughout the process. In fact, if success or failure is only determined after everything has been completed, we may have wasted countless resources only to realize a small adjustment early on may have resulted in a better outcome. Establishing benchmarks in the planning phase of your organizational change will enable you to make the necessary adjustments along the way.

The process whereby organizational leaders can identify the success or failure of change starts with an idealized end in mind. Sometimes identifying that ideal goal or vision is extremely challenging, but once it has been determined, you are ready to establish your process. Dreaming is cheap, so dream big about what needs to be accomplished. Surround yourself with people who know how to dream with you. (When you read that, certain people came to mind that you need to avoid, and others probably came to mind who you would consider dreamers. Keep that list ready, as you will need it later.) This stage of the process is where many people fail before they begin because they dream too small. I cannot emphasize enough the necessity for prayer during this part of the process. I believe that God is interested in what your dreams are (even if they seem less than spiritual at times). Bring all things to Him.

Throughout the dream phase, you should include benchmarks that will accurately measure your accomplishments. It is by these benchmarks that you will determine success or failure throughout the process rather than waiting until the process or change is realized. Few organizations have the luxury of investing resources (people, time, and money) just to see if something is going to be effective. If you fail to reach the first benchmark you set, do not hesitate to rework the plan. It is better to measure the change as ineffective early on so you can make adjustments. No change process should be considered a failure unless the leadership fails to accurately measure the progress. Making adjustments throughout the change process should be considered a normal part of the process. Adjusting the plan to fix a potential problem is not failure; it should be considered a success because the end goal will be much different if you allow your team to make changes along the way.

Identifying Success and Failure in Organizational Change

The success or failure of change should be easily recognized in any organization if the leadership has adequately and openly promoted, encouraged, and weighed the outcome according to the projected results. Simply put, the success or failure of any strategic plan for change should be readily identified by everyone in the organization by asking the question, "Did it work or not?" Doesn't exactly sound earth shattering, does it?

This is not rocket science; it takes no advanced degree or eons of experience to determine the success or failure of any effort. The problem in identifying the success or failure of the change is realized in knowing what the projected outcome was supposed to be. Of course, if the leadership is directing the change agents within their organizations, they will know what changes are projected and which ones are in process, as well as the success or failure of each one. This seldom happens because far too many leaders don't make the investment of time and talent to direct the change; they'd rather sit back and see what happens.

Another problem commonly associated with this matter is the fear many leaders have in revealing the successes (which may lead to complacency) or failures (which may reflect negatively on the leadership). Don't fall into this trap. A willingness to accept both the positive and negative outcomes of any plan for change and a willingness to openly discuss the successes and failures with your employees will go a long way in building morale and squelching the rumor mill. All of us make wise and unwise decisions. Accepting the consequences of both with your employees will ultimately lead to a greater level of respect and trust.

Planning for change is the key to being able to identify the success or failure of organizational change. Planning requires measurable goals and objectives. This enables leadership to manage the progress or regress throughout the change process accordingly rather than waiting for the end results. A measurable process can be frightening to some leaders. It means they will be held accountable for what happens (or what does not happen).

Taking the time to invest in your plan for change will instill confidence and integrity throughout your organizational change. Those working with you throughout the change will learn to trust your authenticity. If you are not afraid to admit when you are wrong and admit that things occasionally require adjustments, others will feel the liberty to engage in change processes and realize they will not be required to "nail it" the first time through. Every change process is a learning experience, and when you are learning with your employees, there is always synergy.

Strategic Thinking

Strategic thinking always requires you to ask the "what if?" questions. Strategic thinking is critical thinking. It is thinking with a strategy in mind. While a leader can do this singularly, it is best accomplished communally, and having the right people on the team is just as important as the actual meetings. People who are in-the-box thinkers should be reserved for other tasks because the dreamers you want on this team are out-of-the-box thinkers. These are the people who know how to respectfully push the limit of your organizational guardrails.

To effectively engage in the strategic thinking process, the team needs to focus on the frame of questions used by a detective: who, what, where, when, why, and how? The following list is certainly not exhaustive, but it does grant a starting point for planning strategically:

- Who should be involved in the planning process?
- Who will be affected by this change process, and have we considered that?
- What do we want to accomplish with this change?
- What competencies and skills will be needed to see this change through?
- Where should we begin?
- Where do we hope to be at the end of this change?
- When do we start?
- When should we meet to consider our benchmarks?

- Why are we doing this?
- Why is this a good idea for our organization?
- How will this affect our employees/customers?
- How will we determine the success or failure of this change?
- Other areas to consider are competencies, skills, products, strengths, weaknesses, environment, industry, overall impact, structure, and alignment with mission and vision.

If you have formulated a winning team, this list will not even scratch the surface of what will be covered in your strategic thinking efforts. Many leaders become so enamored with the idea of change and what it could accomplish for the organization, they tend to skimp on the strategic thinking process. Failure to invest resources in this first part of the change process will require more investment later on. Invest the time, money, and people on the front end to secure adequate buy-in for the duration of the change process.

Strategic thinking is a lot like strategic dreaming—it costs very little compared to the overall organizational impact it may create. Fostering an environment whereby this strategic thinking team can prosper is a critical consideration for organizational leaders. The idea is not to just complete an exercise. Christian leaders should understand the necessity of allowing the Holy Spirit to work in the group and through each team member. When I do this, I do not want a team to sit down and have a plan in one meeting. I want them to banter back and forth, to process and reconsider everything they are sure of. This is the laboratory for strategic planning, and I want maximum input with maximum effort. The changes they will consider will affect our present and our future; therefore, I want to ensure I have pulled out all the stops for this team to excel.

Strategic Planning

Strategic planning often refers to that process organizations use to determine 1) where they want to be headed; 2) where they are headed; and 3) how to correct their course. I am an advocate for this organizational process and believe it should be used throughout our organizations. I believe that we often miss opportunities to include strategic planning in other areas of organizational life and believe we should encourage it in all we do. When an organization has determined to change a process, procedure, product, etc., strategic planning should be an early consideration.

Once again, I employ the team mentality approach, but this time the team is mostly senior level managers, directors, and department leaders, in short, the leaders of the organization. The primary reason for this is these are the people responsible for implementing the change. If something goes awry, this is the group that will have to answer for the missteps. This group may include some dreamers, but I want my analytic minds developing the timeline for implementation, troubleshooting, and action.

Strategic planning is critical planning; it is planning with a strategy. This is not just conceptualizing ideas but making the dreams become reality. Tell this group to actualize the dream, tweak it if they must, but make it happen. This is not an exhaustive list, but it includes some of the key components to consider when developing a strategic planning process (the list works well whether you are considering an organizational strategy or a change strategy for a particular process or project).

- Consider the details. Take the time to deliberate every aspect you are considering.
- Be careful not to get stuck trying to perfect your plan. Internal and external factors change all the time, so every strategic plan should be fluid.

- Develop a SWOT (strengths, weaknesses, opportunities, and threats) chart as a ready reference when planning the details.

- Be clear when identifying your objectives (ideals) and your SMART (specific, measurable, achievable/acceptable, relevant, and timely) goals.

- Determine a defining statement that considers your SWOT analysis and your SMART goals.

- Develop an evaluation process to be used at your benchmarks in determining your stage-by-stage success or failure.

- Strategic planning always considers the investment. Developing an accurate budget for this process is critical, and knowing who is responsible for completing each step is crucial to success.

There are countless resources available for developing a strategic plan, and this was in no way an attempt to include that entire process. My primary objective for including this is to give you a list of things to consider in your change processes.

Organizational change can be minute, or it can be monumental. Taking to the time to carefully consider every change as a make or break opportunity only serves to more adequately prepare your leadership team and your employees to see change as lifegiving rather than life-taking. If leaders take the time to consider every change process in the same manner, their followers will come to fully understand how change should be handled organizationally every time. Every time you invest the resources to process change (in the big things and the small things), you are investing in the long-term health and life of your organization. Waiting until a big change is required to introduce the process will be too late. Do it now, and do it often.

Try It!

1. Would you consider yourself a change embracer or a change avoider? Why?

   _____

   _____

   _____

   _____

   _____

2. Considering the history of your leadership, would you say you are more likely to be a revolutionary change leader or an evolutionary change leader? Why?

_____

_____

_____

_____

_____

CHAPTER 8 Innovating Leader

As we begin this chapter, it is imperative that we reduce the term "innovation" to its most basic definition. Countless numbers of men and women much more gifted than I am have spent chapters and books defining and redefining this term much to the chagrin of those trying to understand it. In its most basic form, innovation means to tap into the creativity, discovery, and invention of a thought, idea, or product and improve upon it. This means I can be an innovator simply by taking your idea and making it better or better suited for my purposes. Many confuse innovation with creativity and discovery. While being innovative may include those elements, each of them stand alone and have their own particular place in a Christian leader's toolbox. The world is full of innovators. Your organization is full of innovators. Recognizing innovation as a God-given gift and understanding the value of how it can be used in your

Portrait of a Christian Leader

organization is a crucial element to rising above the status quo.

All of us practice innovation in our organizations. We do it so often that there is a tendency to overlook what we have done. We order something and modify it to better suit our needs, or perhaps we read an article about how a process works for one of our competitors and we realize it will work even better for us if we add this or alter that. As Christian leaders, innovation is at the heart of our relationship with Christ. He takes me in my basic form, adds some things, removes some things, and makes me better suited for His purposes. It happens so often, so subtly day by day that we often fail to make the connection.

Once we recognize innovation for what it is, we can begin processes to enhance what is already happening. Those processes include intentionality, people, research, and practical approaches to making innovation something we regularly practice as opposed to something that just occasionally occurs in our lives.

Evidence-Based Innovation

At first thought, it may seem like an oxymoron to pursue evidence-based innovation. Things that are evidence-based have been tried, tested, and proven, which seems to be counter to innovation. Innovation screams of ingenuity, creativity, and all the things that are edgy and spur of the moment. To be able to marry these terms and see them in action is an exciting process indeed. It is possible to prove out our innovations and not stifle creativity, but it will come with a cost.

Practicing evidence-based innovation will require you to invest in the process of innovation and evidence-based management individually and then make a concentrated effort to marry the two. This is where the cost comes. Evidence-based management requires us to invest in our planning on the front end of the change. That is, to do our homework and research the hows and whys before we ever invest any effort to make a change. Consequently, innovation done right requires leadership to make a concerted effort in creating time and opportunity for our employees to practice innovation. While there are costs, they are best viewed as an investment.

Rather than allowing an innovation team the freedom to just run with their ideas and innovations, senior leadership should invest in the time necessary to assess the success of an innovation before implementation. It may seem an unnecessary step to make this declaration, but it is not as far-fetched as you may think. I can personally attest to the countless hours of wasted manpower and expenses associated with practicing innovation as opposed to practicing evidence-based innovation. Allow the creativity, the ideas, the innovations to come alive, but allow those teams that develop innovative ideas to carry it one step further and research the feasibility and practicality of those innovations before going any further.

This creates a certain level of accountability with your innovation team. It is no longer the team's responsibility to just create ideas and come up with new ways of doing things or affecting your business. It encourages the team to think through their ideas before they go any further. It encourages the team to act responsibly and offer innovations that will produce positive results as opposed to just looking good on paper or sounding great in a meeting. It compels them to prove the question, "Will it work?" before anyone ever hears about it.

Diagnosing Innovation Issues

It is usually easy to recognize those individuals who have a knack for innovation. They think outside the box. They look at the same things as everyone else, but they see them differently. Natural innovators are wired differently. While all of us possess some level of innovative ability, there are others who just seem to be predisposed to it. When those people are not being innovative, when they are not expressing their creativity, something is wrong. If those natural innovators are not contributing, it is likely that others in the organization are not being very innovative either.

If leaders want to foster innovation, they must be intentional in creating those opportunities. Creating an environment whereby innovation naturally occurs within the organizational culture compels leadership to know how their team members are wired. Do you know your people? Do you know what their passions are? What are their causes? We all have them—you know those things, those areas that we are anxious to talk about and process with others. Innovators typically only need a cause. Pull them together and share a problem that you have recognized but struggle with and watch what happens. It is common for innovators to have a passion to want to *fix* things for leadership. They may want to do that because they enjoy or thrive on the compliments that often accompany their ideas and innovation. Often, it is simply having the opportunity to make a difference.

If innovation is not naturally occurring, it could be that you or the leadership team has stifled it. Ask yourself these questions:

- Have I taken the time to really listen to someone today?
- Have I been overly concentrated on myself lately?
- Have I been open and honest about the organizational struggles we are facing?
- Do I shoot down the ideas of others before they have a chance to share them?
- Do I have a plan in place to strategically utilize my innovators?
- Have I neglected the plan I created to utilize my innovators?
- Do I carry the weight of the organizational problems or do I share them?

- When was the last time I asked someone else to fix an organizational issue?

This is only a starting point. You know which questions to ask to compel you to recognize a problem. I encourage you to always look at yourself and your leadership team first when diagnosing innovation issues. Those who are predisposed to innovative thought processes will always be practicing it at some level (they cannot seem to help themselves), so if you do not notice them being innovative, perhaps it's because you are distracted or your leadership team is preoccupied.

If you recognize innovation is lacking in your culture, consider creating times that encourage departments and individuals to come together for the sole purpose of being innovative. Give the team a simple problem to tackle and watch how they respond to it. Gradually increase the difficulty and eventually have the team address a real-time problem the organization is facing. Leaders should be willing to be vulnerable when doing this. Let the team know that you need them to creatively address this issue. Tell them you are depending on them to address this problem. Hold them accountable for creating a solution. Set a time to sit down with them and hear their solution. There is a synergy that is created when those with the ability to fix a problem are empowered to do so and then held accountable for the assessment of their idea.

If you have identified that the team is working and that organizational leadership is not the problem and yet innovation is still lacking, you must carefully consider how much time, energy, and money you are willing to invest in order to jump-start the process. It could be that a particular department or area of the organization needs some additional help. One of the things that may encourage innovation is spending time with this group aside from their normal duties at the organization. Consider the following:

- Schedule a special meeting for this group/department with an outside motivational speaker.
- Take this group to dinner and be willing to share your concerns.
- Plan a retreat for this group that will incorporate the first two ideas.
- Mix the group up and bring in someone from another department.

It is important to recognize that this group most likely wants to help with the problem, they just are not sure how.

Berating them and creating impossible scenarios for them to consider seldom fosters innovation and often serves to further stifle it. Be patient with this team and watch what will happen.

Since this is a book about Christian leadership, I cannot overemphasize the necessity of prayer. It would be a rare occurrence to find an organization run by Christian leaders where the entire workforce is entirely made up of Christians. Consequently, the way you introduce prayer to the innovation process must be gentle and considerate. This means we never force others to participate in the process of prayer, but we should never apologize for it either. Fundamentally, it comes down to believing that God can help or not. If we believe He can help with this process, then we would be amiss to not ask Him. If we do not believe He can handle this request, then as *Christian* leaders, we have a much larger issue to deal with.

Christian leaders should pray that they will exemplify a healthy, open relationship with Jesus Christ. Christian leadership teams should pray that they would know and respond to the heart of God as it pertains to their business. Innovation teams being directed by Christian leaders should always include prayer as a part of the processes they employ.

Portrait of a Christian Leader

Far too often, we are Christian in name only. That means we like the name and use the name when it is convenient, and this is a disgrace to the cause of Christ. Either we are Christians all the time or we are Christians none of the time.

Consequently, we should include Him in every arena of our lives: rejoicing in the reality of His presence on Sunday morning, Monday's briefing, Tuesday afternoon, Wednesday evening, at Thursday's meeting, and Friday's luncheon. If we are experiencing a void of innovative ideas, we should always ask Him for help first.

If you lead or are part of an organization where being vocal about your faith is not encouraged or allowed, understand that you are still a Christian leader. You can still pray and ask God to intervene in your situation even if it is when you are alone or before you arrive at work each day. I have watched Him create authentic Christian community in secular workplaces in creative and unique ways. If we will endeavor to welcome Him as part of the process (publicly or privately), He will show up.

Using Innovation to Improve Organizations

If you are not sold on the process of intentional innovation by now, here are a few additional things for you to consider. Leaders enslaved to a regimen, plan, or approach will become myopic. In doing so, they hinder their own ability to lead and their organization from becoming all it could be. Innovative processes empower us to break out of those prisons of "the same old, same old." Practicing innovation compels us to move from the comforts of commonality to the creativity of nonconformity.

Most forward-thinking leaders would agree there is nothing you are currently doing that cannot be done better. More production, more revenue, more involvement, and more customers are just a few of the things that could be better. Seeing innovation as a tool to improve everything you do as opposed to another organizational fad to exploit will help you get on the right track. No matter their level of education, experience, or knowledge of a process or product, your employees are the key to using innovation to improve your organization. Whether you are the sole employee or your organization employs hundreds of people, tapping into that creativity is the key to improving your organization and creating change.

Some of the things I have already mentioned that may assist in this process include: developing an innovation team, setting aside a specific time each week or month when this team comes together for the sole purpose of practicing and refining the innovative process, scheduling off-hours gatherings for this team to interact with one another, and scheduling an innovation retreat. Any one of these ideas sends a loud message to your employees that innovation is important, expected, and celebrated in your organization. You may want to consider adding a section to your annual employee reviews that will measure the employee's reaction and response to innovation.

It is time to sacrifice the sacred cows and throw a party in honor of innovation. A leader who is secure enough to lay everything on the table and encourage his or her employees to improve on everything being done will most certainly be rewarded with an improved organization and active, involved employees. Leaders who like to micromanage and control the environments in their organizations will find this idea reckless and scary. Consequently, this type of leader will grow increasingly antiquated in the twenty-first century.

Innovating Leader

I served under a well-respected leader one time who was an expert micromanager. He had his finger on literally everything that was happening in his organization. While some may see that as responsible leadership, those serving under his leadership were greatly hindered, and creativity that was not birthed by him was constantly stifled. The workplace was stagnant. Little to no innovation was practiced because it threatened this insecure leader. As it was, every part of this organization suffered.

Providing a culture that encouraged innovation would have improved this organization. Rather than becoming dependent on the insights and experiences of one person, the company would have benefitted from the insights and experiences of the other one hundred or so employees. Innovation relies on the creativity of the group and the synergy that is created when multiple ideas are mixed together. No one person can lead alone in the twenty-first century. We need teams and creativity and innovation to be the new norm, not the anomaly they have so often become.

Innovation is seeing old things, old processes, and old ideas through a new set of lenses. Those of you who wear glasses understand this analogy perfectly. There are times when working outside or, more specifically, when

Portrait of a Christian Leader

woodworking that my glasses become so dust-covered, I can no longer see clearly. Of course, I seldom recognize that right away. I may rub my eyes, turn on a light, and maybe even move my project to a different location before I realize I need to clean my glasses. The truth is I am so focused on what I must do that I forget to do what I need to do: clean my glasses.

The same is true of leaders who fail to recognize the value of supporting innovation to improve their organization. Rather than making the organization all about us, we need to creatively find ways to include others in the process. You have a mind and they have a mind, so working together on the same project will enable you to see things through different sets of lenses and process things with different experiences and insights. This then is a win-win situation! Imagine for a moment what intentionally practicing innovation could do for your organization, your leadership, and your employees. What are you waiting for?

Try It!

Through the process of reading this chapter, perhaps you may have discovered that innovation is not one of your strengths. The easiest thing to do would be to ignore this chapter and think this was for someone else. As a Christian leader, practicing innovation is essential. Typically, the Christian community operates about fifteen to twenty years behind the secular community in terms of creativity and out-of-the-box thinking. Even if you are not an innovator in the truest sense, practicing innovation in your workplace is possible. If you dare to dream and believe that God can use innovation to improve your organization, walk through this exercise and ask Him for faith to believe this can be a reality for you and your company.

1. List a few of the areas in which you have practiced innovation or areas that need an innovative touch.

   _____

   _____

2. Who would you consider the top three to seven innovators in your organization?

   a. _____

   b. _____

   c. _____

   d. _____

Portrait of a Christian Leader

e. _____

f. _____

g. _____

CHAPTER 9 Coaching Leader

Let me begin by declaring that leadership coaching is not counseling, mentoring, or discipling. Coaching may incorporate some aspects of each of those areas, but it stands alone in terms of its scope and projected outcomes and what it can accomplish. Much like a coach of some sport or athletic activity, a leadership coach should bring out the best in us. There were times when I played on an organized sports team and I would get frustrated, aggravated, and just want to give up (or go pick a fight). More times than not, my coach would pull me aside and help me to get refocused. He would push me to the limit in order to make me a better athlete. Leadership coaches today do that and more. A well-structured plan, fully actuated in a leader's life, will enable that individual to go places he or she could never go alone.

Coaching is not counseling. The primary focus of counseling is deciphering one's past in order to move forward. Counseling may include deep sessions uncovering hidden issues, medication, and prolonged encounters with a licensed professional in order to discover why things are as they are. The primary objective of coaching is looking forward, not looking back.

Coaching is not mentoring. A mentor is someone who takes you where he or she has been based on their life experience. It is not uncommon for an organization to assign a mentor to a new employee for the purpose of *teaching the new person the ropes* of the organization. Every organization has its own unique set of norms—those things that are often unwritten, but a part of the organization's culture. A mentor shows the mentee the path through the ins and outs of those norms in order to provide the proper foundation for their success. If you have been assigned a mentor, that mentor normally only informs you of the things that he or she has experienced.

Coaching is not discipleship. In the truest form of the word, discipleship is helping someone to look more like Jesus Christ. The person who disciples will often guide, prod, and direct the one being discipled through the process

Coaching Leader

of developing Christlikeness. As Jesus directs, the one who leads the discipleship process guides the one being discipled through the disciplines of the Christian faith.

In its most basic form, coaching is helping a person get from where they are to where they need to be through guided discussion and accountability. A coach does not have to have all the right answers or be more informed than the person being coached. A coach pulls out the best in you; he or she helps you to get moving and progress toward your goal. The coach does not set the agenda, but allows the person being coached to determine where he or she wants (or needs) to go and then assists them with developing a process to get there.

Every Christian leader should be a coach. We see elements of coaching qualities and traits throughout the earthly ministry of Jesus Christ. He held His ground and determined to guide, prod, and direct the affairs of the individuals around Him, while discipling them. A Christian leader who has not developed nor intentionally focused on the coaching aspect of his or her leadership has been missing an opportunity to positively impact his or her team members toward lasting and beneficial change. Coaching will require you to really know your employees and then use that knowledge to motivate them to greater heights and deeper depths. Intentionally coaching your employees will enhance every aspect of your organization and their professional development.

Coaching Leaders

In his book entitled *Leadership Coaching: The Disciplines, Skills, and Heart of a Christian Coach,* Tony Stoltzfus states that, "To be an effective leader means being a coach." [5] Senior leaders influence the way business is done and the progress and productivity of their teams; virtually everything an organization does or does not do is influenced and affected by those who lead. Leaders who fail to recognize this detail and fail to measure the impact of their leadership in their organizations will never see their business reach its full potential.

Every leader is a coach. You may not be actively engaged in the coaching process, but those around you are learning from you. It is a most sobering moment when a leader realizes that he or she has not been modeling the correct things for their employees. Most of us have had the unfortunate experience of serving with leaders who taught us more about what not to do as opposed to what we should be doing. Set a personal goal today to not be that type of leader.

Leaders who coach their employees must be willing to engage at a deeper level than they may be accustomed to. Coaches should have a relationship with the person being coached that goes beyond the chain of command. Because this element is crucial for effective coaching, many leaders avoid it. It can be intimidating for some folks to let their guards down. You know how it is: "I am the leader in this organization; people must see me in a certain way, and I must never appear vulnerable or without an answer." Leaders who live like this are miserable people. It is a terrible responsibility to feel as if you must have the right answer or the right words all the time. Coaching involves authenticity, and being real with your team members does not make you a lesser leader. Leaders who make coaching a priority pass along strategies to their team on how to lead rather than just follow. We are all followers by nature; we do that from the earliest days of our lives. We tag along behind Mom, Dad, or an older sibling and do what they do. Making followers is not a difficult process; making good leaders is a difficult process and it starts with coaching.

Coaching is an investment in the productivity, effectiveness, and efficiency of the organization, one person at a time. When I coach an individual, I am not just helping him or her become better equipped to do a job, I am teaching them to equip everyone they encounter. I may be helping to improve the individual's performance, but the investment also will pay huge dividends in the way that person interacts with others, performs his or her job, and meets organizational objectives, and how that person will coach others under his or her influence in the future.

Establishing Trust

Trust must be present first in order to create an effective coaching atmosphere. Trust is not something you can create, purchase, or manufacture. It begins the day a potential employee is interviewed. It includes elements of honesty, forthrightness, integrity, openness, and vulnerability. Simply creating an illusion where people can feel trust and creating an environment where trust permeates the culture are two different things. As a leader, I must first ensure that trust is present in my organization before I can begin building on trust in individual relationships.

To coach is to be trustworthy. If you have not proven yourself to be trustworthy to those around you, you cannot expect a coaching relationship to just automatically create trust. Leaders who have not been trustworthy will find an uphill battle in becoming effective coaches to their employees. The focus of this section is not to help you re-create trust when trust has been broken as that topic goes beyond the scope of this book. My goal with this section is to encourage the Christian leader to create a culture of trustworthiness in their organization and use that as a springboard to effective coaching.

Can you keep a confidence? Have you followed through with what you said you would do? Have others shared intimate details of their lives, struggles, and victories with you? All these point to a culture of trust. If leaders will coach those around them, those around them must not sense they are being evaluated or judged when talking about life issues. Coaching serves to address behaviors, challenges, and seemingly insurmountable obstacles in order to become a more effective leader. You will never be afforded an opportunity to do that if those around you feel like you cannot be trusted.

Establishing trust is a crucial first step when coaching others. I have used a variety of techniques to do this with others, and each time my attempts to do so have been intentional. You cannot establish trust with a lackadaisical attitude. Creating an atmosphere of trust is crucial to the success of your employees and your organization because failure to coach your subordinates is failure—period. These people who come to work each day are not there to simply get a paycheck. Everyone wants to make a difference in what they are doing. Coaching enables you to help them become more efficient and effective in what they are already doing, which in turn should increase overall organizational productivity. Better employees make for a better organization, and coaching is a great way to accomplish both.

Maintaining Integrity

Simply put, integrity is maintaining moral uprightness whether someone is watching you or not. As Christians, we understand that God never slumbers or sleeps (Psalm 121:4); He is always watching. We live in a time when double standards and falsities are the norm. If I pretend to be an ethical person today and look for ways to beat the system tomorrow, I am not a person of integrity.

Integrity addresses matters of the heart. Politicians often find themselves the butt of many jokes based on a perceived lack of integrity. They may act concerned about an issue if it garnishes votes and then flip that perspective to a different crowd in order to gain their votes. Acting in this manner is a gross lack of integrity. When it comes to coaching those around you, maintaining your integrity is crucial. Coaching is personal; it requires that you deal with things that are often very personal in nature. If you express concern over those issues with your employees in a coaching moment and then use those vulnerabilities or weaknesses to your advantage later, you have blown your integrity.

If the people you coach perceive a lack of integrity, your coaching will not be very effective. Integrity that has been built up over time can be destroyed or damaged in an instant. It is not difficult to create a feeling of integrity, but maintaining it is hard work and well worth the effort you will expend in doing so. Just as you cannot coach effectively without trust, you cannot build trust without integrity. When you have integrity, treat it as a costly jewel. Protect it, nurture it, and maintain it at all costs.

Portrait of a Christian Leader

Building a Model for Christian Leadership Coaching

We live in a time where organizational loyalty is not a very high priority for most people. By that statement, I mean that folks will be loyal as long as they perceive you are loyal to them. If their perception is distorted (it matters not whether they are right or wrong in their perception), they will be gone. The days are long past when we could expect an employee to come to our organization as a young man or woman and stay there until retirement. Nevertheless, an effective model for Christian leadership coaching can curtail that trend and possibly even reverse it. We should do everything in our power to attract and keep the best employees we can get. Each day they spend working for us, they are building time and experience in their positions. They make mistakes and learn from those mistakes. When they decide to leave, we are forced to start the process all over again with someone new. Christian leaders who establish a model for Christian coaching in their organizations will see lasting, positive change. The idea with building a model for Christian leadership coaching should be to see every employee ultimately involved in a coaching relationship. If this is a new process for you, pace yourself. It may seem like an insurmountable goal to accomplish this; however, creating a model will enable you to set a precedent for the future. You are not building this model to simply satisfy a checklist in a book; this is about the present health and future growth of your organization. Consider these steps as you make your plans:

1. **Be fully convinced that leadership coaching is the best approach for your organization.**

   As a primary leader in your organization or department, the first thing you need to do is be fully convinced that leadership coaching is the best way for your organization to advance. If you are not fully convinced that this is the way you should go, you will find yourself questioning everything and looking for a way out right from the start. Coaching helps your employees become better in every area of their lives. That, in turn, will make your employees better suited and equipped in their jobs. There are many things you can do to help your organization become more profitable and effective in your market, and this is one of them. Coaching is not simply a quick fix to better the business. It is a way of investing in your people by recognizing they are truly your most valuable assets. If someone gave you a million dollars to make your organization better, you could easily spend that by building this, buying that, improving systems, enhancing products and services, etc. When all was said and done, you would have one million dollars' worth of improvements, and hopefully you would get more than one million dollars' worth of return on your investment. However, when you invest in coaching your employees, it is impossible to gauge the value you are creating. How can you gauge the worth of an employee who becomes a better person? How can you determine the value of a better father, a better wife, or a better middle-level manager? There is no way to determine the value. When you personally invest your time and resources into your people, you create organic synergy, and no amount of money can purchase that.

2. **Find a coach who will help you accomplish the goal of building a model for Christian leadership coaching.**

For you to effectively build and facilitate an effective coaching model for your organization, you need to understand the basics of the coaching industry. A coach who will guide you through the process and help you map out a strategy for your business will prove invaluable. The primary notion behind this step is to build a coaching model that will enhance your employees and grow your organization. Do not necessarily settle for the first coach you contact. Finding the right person to guide you through this process is crucial to the success of the coaching model. The idea is to not just find the right coach, but the right *Christian* coach. You will want to build your model on the principles of the Bible and the ministry of Jesus Christ.

3. **Use the life of Jesus as your guide.**

You are a Christian who happens to be a leader of a group of people. As such, you should always defer to the Bible as your guide for life and conduct. Jesus was given many titles in Scripture, and I would like to add another one now: Coach. The way Jesus built His relationship with the disciples and His means of interaction and compelling them to action exemplifies that of a Christian coach extraordinaire. Jesus used questions in order to motivate those around Him to think through the issues of life. He held His followers accountable for their thoughts, actions, and inactions. His ability to do this effectively has played out in the years since His death on the cross. We are products of His coaching model. He engaged His followers, and as a result of living with, walking with, and dying for His cause, His followers established a lasting model for Christian leadership coaching.

4. **Define your organization.**

Develop a written mission statement, a vision statement, and core values that will become the foundation of your coaching model. These components do not come easily. It takes time and effort to bring them to life, and in doing so, you are preparing the organization to grow beyond your own leadership skills. Included in the coaching model should be the key components of why you do what you do. By reiterating these elements in your coaching model, you are empowering your employees to make decisions based on who the organization is and where it is headed, rather than on what they think is a good idea. If you do not use a structured plan, you are expecting all your employees to automatically be on the same page with the same goals and objectives. They cannot accomplish that unless there is a plan in place.

This is by no means an exhaustive list of how you can establish an effective model for leadership coaching; it is simply a starting point. The leadership coach you hire to help you build this model for Christian leadership coaching in your organization will need these elements to get the process started. I cannot overstate the benefits of hiring a leadership coach for your organization. This needs to be an annual part of your budget allocation. This is not to say that you will be paying for coaching services all year long. However, most leaders will need someone to assist them in the start-up phase. It is also a good idea to bring that individual in from time to time to make sure you are staying on track. Following through with this process is not just accumulating another expense; it is investing in the future of your organization and the men and women who will make it great.

Portrait of a Christian Leader

Why Accountability is Important

Even the best laid plans often find themselves in the dustbins of our lives. We plan, organize, and coordinate the necessary steps to have a successful organization. We do this with our personal lives too: diets, finances, raising children, etc. All of this, and somewhere along the way, life happens and we get distracted. Things break, conflicts emerge, personalities get too big, and we lose our way. It does not matter how well structured our plans are, this will happen. Having an independent party, someone not intimately connected with the details of our plans or organizations, will prove invaluable to ensuring the success of our organization.

No matter how strong of a leader you may be, you are still human. Human beings get side-tracked, waylaid, and confused. No matter how well I have conditioned myself spiritually, I still find myself becoming easily distracted from following Christ. Even though I realize He is the life force behind all I do and I understand how much I depend on Him for my very breath, all it takes is one bad moment and I find myself trying to take over my life again. The individuals God has brought into my life are there for a variety of reasons, and one of those reasons is for the purpose of accountability.

I need them to ask me the tough questions and remind me to stay properly focused. Without their gentle nudging, prodding, and love, I will never be all that He intended me to be. A coach holds those he or she is coaching accountable. The people God has brought into my life all serve as coaches in some capacity in that they hold me accountable for what I do, what I say, and how I act. Those who serve as accountability partners are not always welcomed into our lives, for sometimes their words are hard and challenging—but we need them.

The Christian leader as coach will hold his or her subordinates accountable for their actions, their words, and their organizational involvement. Holding someone accountable with intentionality is not an easy job. At times, it requires you to hold a hand, hug a shoulder, and maybe even provide a good, swift kick (well, maybe not too swift). When I hold you accountable, I am showing you that I care. I care enough to get in your face and even be a pest if need be to get you heading in the right direction again.

Portrait of a Christian Leader

Coaches always serve as accountability partners. Once again, Stoltzfus says that "... accountability is standing in for God." [6] Seeing accountability in this way elevates the magnitude of coaching our followers. I coach my employees and hold them accountable because, in doing so, I am telling them how important they are to me and our organization. I do not want them to get off track personally because not only will they suffer, but their performance at work will also likely suffer as well. If I do not hold them accountable for what they do while at work, I am telling them that the job they perform is unimportant to me. I have encountered countless leaders who will say that they care for their employees and the employees never see evidence of that. On the other hand, when you enter a workplace where the employees have felt the love and care of their leaders, a synergy is present. We all need accountability. Why not make it a regular part of the benefits your employees receive when working for your organization?

Try It!

Coaching requires time and investment. It is not something you can delegate to someone else and hope it happens. As a leader, your employees need you to coach them. They want to do a good job for you. They want to grow in their knowledge and involvement. They want to see the organization become more profitable and competitive. If these statements do not epitomize your organization, it may be because you have not taken the initiative to coach your employees to the next level.

I have barely scratched the surface of the coaching industry; nevertheless, I hope I have provided enough to get you thinking about it. A coaching model that actively engages your employees may be the catalyst you need to propel your organization to the next level, so try it!

1. List the people in your life who have coached you or whom you have coached in some capacity.

   a. _____

   b. _____

   c. _____

   d. _____

   e. _____

   f. _____

Portrait of a Christian Leader

2. What are some things you have learned from previous leaders that you do not want to duplicate?

_____

_____

_____

_____

CHAPTER 10 Initiating Leader

There have been countless times in my life as a leader that I have complained about the fact that no one was being creative or that we were just sitting still as an organization. Complaining, finger-pointing, and fault finding are the traits of a weak leader. It was not until I realized it was my responsibility to be the initiator that I had a different perspective. As a Christian leader, you are the initiator. You are responsible for getting things started. Expecting someone else to do it is an exercise in futility.

The same Spirit that hovered over the waters in Genesis 1:1 is alive in you. The Holy Spirit is the ultimate initiator. He brings life, creativity, and ingenuity to individuals and to organizations. It is not uncommon for leaders to isolate, hesitate, and fail to initiate out of a lack of confidence or fear of the unknown. Nevertheless, when we allow Him to work in us and through us as leaders, we should be in motion. Motion is the lifeblood of an organization where He is allowed the freedom to move and bring things into existence. He is the initiator, and He lives in you. The lives of your organization and the people who work there are depending on your ability to yield to His guiding presence—don't blow it!

Understanding Your Role as a Christian Leader

If you have not already noticed, God is seldom welcomed in corporate board meetings, training sessions, and the daily activities of the modern workplace. If He is recognized, it is usually so He can be blamed for something. Your role as a Christian leader is to make Him evident in everything you touch. That means you should expect to see Him in your forecasting, your budget, and your day to day activities. Your employees should come to expect some sign of Him in company functions, break rooms, and the production lines, even if they haven't met Him yet. This does not mean that we become extreme in our presentations of Christian themes and focuses. What it does mean is that we need to work extra hard to ensure His presence is not something that is forced or coerced, but it is something that is natural.

Can you imagine a workplace where the employees can hardly wait to get to work? Rather than longing for the end of the day, what if our employees hated to see the end of the day come? I know this may sound a bit radical, and you may be thinking that would never happen for your organization. If you think creating this type of environment depends solely on your abilities, it will never become a reality. You cannot create this type of environment, but He can. As the Christian leader learns to yield to and work in conjunction with the Holy Spirit, it is possible!

Being a Christian leader is not something we turn on and off. Our relationship with Jesus Christ is not a decoration we add to our lives; it is the very essence of our lives. Rather than wishing something could be done to create better production figures, pray for it! Rather than wandering aimlessly with regards to future direction for the organization, ask Him for direction! You are the initiator. You carry the weight of ensuring He is given full access to your employees, your goals, and your objectives. He will never force His way into your ability to lead; however, rest assured that He longs to be the creative force behind your leadership. He wants to influence your employees and you may be the means He will use to make that happen.

God is interested in your business. He wants to see you succeed and He wants to use the platform of your success to influence others. You can point people to Him by yielding your leadership and your position to the Holy Spirit.

There are many aspects to your role as a Christian leader, but this is without a doubt the most important. Intentionally bringing His influence into the organization may be blatant or subtle, but it must happen, and He has entrusted this responsibility to you. It starts with you including Him in every aspect of your position. This is not intended to imply that you must be public when including Him. Publicly bringing Christ into the workplace can be accomplished, if done in a respectful and honorable way. A leader who is authentic in his or her relationship with Christ will be careful to include Him behind the scenes long before he or she ever tries to do so publicly. Pray. Communicate with Him about your position, your organizational issues, and your employees and expect Him to respond—He will not disappoint you.

Developing Those Under You

Those around you are all the by-products of someone else's leadership. From my experience, it takes about two years

Initiating Leader

until your influence begins to be consistently reflected in the performance of your team. I once spoke with a senior leader in an organization who was commenting on his own leadership style. He told me, "Those around me will not accomplish anything unless I stay on them all the time." He had been there more than ten years! Developing those around you must be a priority; no one else is going to do it. Leaders who complain about the lack of initiative in their employees need to recognize the weight of their influence and, in most cases, should shoulder the responsibility alone.

I wish someone had taught this lesson to me early in life. I have wasted many opportunities to influence members of my team. I would correct them, encourage them, cry with them, laugh with them—everything except intentionally develop them. By the time I learned this lesson, I found myself grieving over wasted days that equated to wasted time and wasted opportunities. Leaders influence those around them whether they are intentional or not; as a result, you might as well be intentional about helping them grow.

We see this lesson taught throughout the Bible. Jesus influenced His disciples, Paul influenced Timothy (and many others), and Moses did the same for Joshua. From these examples, we discover the plan that God had from the beginning was that those in positions of leadership should influence those who follow them. You should seize every opportunity to influence those around you. This is not some haphazard attempt to just be a friend or get them to like you. I am referring to an intentional effort to help them grow to the next level. If you are a confident leader who has taken his or her position seriously, you will encourage those on your team to reach their highest potential. In fact, if every employee rising higher became your goal, you would discover a journey filled with excitement and tremendous fulfillment.

From Daydreams to Realization

Leaders are often encouraged to dream: dream about the possibilities, dream about the potential, and dream about the future. As the primary initiator, one of the keys to success is to move those dreams into realities. I am an advocate for dreaming big dreams. They can be fun, and they are always cheap. However, if we are not careful, we become so proficient at dreaming that we never see them realized. Bringing those dreams alive only happens when you recognize you are the initiator; you are the one to set the wheels in motion and make the dreams become a reality. So, how can you make that happen?

To create something, to make it come alive, requires the opportunity to first dream about it. That will not happen in the organizational environment unless time is intentionally set aside to dream. Investing in a "dream" session can be fun, scary, and addictive. What do you think may happen if you pulled a group of five to seven people together each quarter and invested an hour or two for them to just dream? Many people will think you are nuts, but many employees would be busting down the door to have a shot at it. If you want things to change and you have the power to make those changes, initiate them. It is this kind of out-of-the-box thinking that transforms an organization.

You may not think that kind of idea is realistic in your organization, but you can work around that. Your job as the key initiator is to discover what *is* realistic for your organization and do it. If you find yourself spending time complaining about the lack of creativity or ingenuity in your organization, perhaps you should bear that responsibility (at least in part). Your employees want to dream, they want to see improvements, and they want to be a part of a revolution where dreams become reality. They may be waiting on you to tell them it is okay to dream.

Once the dreaming begins, it is time to take those dreams to the next level. I realize that you cannot take every dream and act on it. If you tried to do that, you would soon be so far off track as an organization that you may have to stop everything and regroup. However, if you select the single strongest dream from each quarterly meeting, imagine what that could do for your organization. This exercise becomes much more than just a fun way to spend a few hours. It could actually give birth to new product line, a new outreach, or a new standard for your business.

As a leader, you have the power to initiate an effort like this (or something else you may dream up) and watch it take shape. You have the influence to empower your employees to contribute to the effort and dream and realize the sky's the limit. There are countless ideas, limitless man hours, and incredible potential at your disposal each day, and they show up in the form of the men and women who compose your workforce. You will never realize that full potential unless you, as the initiator, take action.

Initiating Leader

The role of initiator is one of the most under-utilized roles that a leader has. It is commonplace to spend time and money on programs, events, training, team building, etc., and fail to capitalize on the primary resource your organization has—your employees! If every leader actively engaged his or her role as the initiator, I am confident that today's organizations would look different. Dreams can be fun and stimulating, but they serve little purpose unless actions follow them.

Vulnerability

Many organizations have not had the benefit of having a leader so actively engage their employees in a manner as I have described. Leaders have traditionally offered counsel, provided insight, and led their organizations from a distance. To act as the initiator will require you to be actively engaged with your employees (most of the roles described in this book require this). Like being a coach, being an initiator requires a level of vulnerability that makes many leaders uncomfortable. Your employees need to see you as the servant leader I described in chapter one. If your employees are going to engage in this process of dreaming and actualizing, they will need to see you as supportive of these initiatives.

It is difficult for many leaders to be vulnerable because they are fearful of being rejected (especially Christian leaders). As a result, our insecurities inhibit our organizations and our leadership from becoming all it can be. Learning to be vulnerable is one of the most liberating experiences a leader can have. This is like letting your hair down and allowing your subordinates to see you as a man or woman who struggles and triumphs in the same way they do. The initiator is a key role that needs to be filled. Leaders who fail to find a way to make this role a reality will continue to waste time and miss opportunities. Make every effort to get things started in your organization.

Try It!

The easiest response to this section is to admit you need to initiate change. The most difficult step in becoming an initiator is to actually get something started. I understand how easy it is to fall into the rut of talking about change and never actually changing. This is the reason I included a "Try It!" in each chapter. I want you to be the initiator. As I noted before, things are going to happen in your

Initiating Leader

organization, so you might as well be proactive—dream of the change, work the change, and make the change productive for your business.

1. As a (or the) leader in your organization, what things have you initiated?

   _____

   _____

   _____

   _____

   _____

2. As a Christian leader in your organization, in what ways have you intentionally included God in the workplace?

   _____

   _____

   _____

   _____

   _____

CHAPTER 11 A Final Challenge

When all is said and done and your life is over, someone will most likely eulogize you. They will write down your accomplishments, achievements won, and a number of other nice, positive things that highlight your life on earth. I have been to a few funerals where this has happened, and the things being said did not quite match up with the person I knew. Sometimes, the eulogy was understated, and other times, it was overstated. Perhaps I think too much about such things, but I have often wondered what will be remembered most about my life.

Start Now

Every day, we have an opportunity to affect the way we will be remembered. It happens in the way we serve, lead, and follow. Time seems to be moving at a breakneck rate, and we cannot afford to waste any of it. I encourage leaders to make a list of the things they want to be remembered for. Then, as they evaluate their lives and leadership, they should honestly consider whether those things show up. It is not uncommon to have a great gap between who you think you are, and the person others actually see. Making an impact does not start next year or when you get that promotion; it has already happened and will continue to happen in the days that follow.

Coming to grips with the reality that your eulogy is being written today should serve as a motivator to be the best person, the best leader, the best Christian you can possibly be each day. To delay in this action is to fail. Words spoken in haste, actions meted out in a rush, and thoughts carelessly becoming words all live in infamy in the minds of those who are around us each day. The urgency of the day cannot be expressed enough. Today you will encounter people, speak words of death or life into them, and make decisions that will outlive you. Whether those things adequately depict the person you are or not, they may be the only things some folks ever remember.

As I write that, I think of those who have been adversely affected by my careless leadership over the years. In this case, time has not served to erase those memories. In fact,

A Final Challenge

time has served to reinforce what I have done wrong. I am hopeful that my eulogy will include the things that are most meaningful to me. Nevertheless, for some, the pain of the poor leadership they have followed in the past will serve as a constant reminder of who they should have been.

Every Christian leader should desire to finish well. Regardless of how we started the race, how many stumbles we experienced, how many falls we took, and how many casualties we have been responsible for, all of us want to finish well. Finishing well is a goal we can set at any time of our careers; we all have a chance to lead well and support others. However, it is best to start your journey as early as possible. If you look back over your life and career and see only shortcomings in performance, take the time now and determine to finish well. Change starts today.

Accountability Team

Having people in your life who love you enough to get in your face often and for the right reasons is invaluable. It takes time to develop an accountability team that understands who you are on your good days and your bad days. You might have a list of people who are eager to tell you what to do, but they are not the folks you need on your accountability team. You need people who know you. Those with whom you have been vulnerable and genuine. These people understand your goals, your dreams, and your strengths and weaknesses. So how can you determine who should be a part of your team?

1. Choose people you respect. You should never ask someone to hold you accountable if you do not value his or her perspective.

2. Choose those who know you. They have been witnesses of your mistakes and beneficiaries of your talents. They have seen the good, the bad, and the ugly of your leadership (and life) and have not left. They know your likes, dislikes, your family, and your history. You need people like this on your team because they know what you are capable of handling.

3. Do not let age be a concern. When choosing an accountability team, it would not be uncommon to pick those friends or colleagues who are close to your age. If a younger or older person fits the other criteria, do not hesitate to ask them for their help.

A Final Challenge

A wide range in ages, backgrounds, and education will assist you in gaining perspective and insight.

4. Pray. One of the simplest yet least developed tools in a Christian leader's toolbox is prayer. By asking God to guide this process, you are relying on His wisdom as opposed to your own. You are also intentionally including Him in the decisions of your life. He has your best interest at heart and choosing to include Him honors His influence in your life.

Self-Evaluation

Many leadership gurus have prepared tests, tools, and assessments to assist leaders in self-evaluation. These tests help us to chart a course, get on track, and stay there for a while. I am an advocate for a tool like this that works in helping us become better leaders. I have benefitted from these things in my leadership, and I believe they can provide great value.

I have not developed a test to measure your potential or gauge your weaknesses. However, I do have a series of questions designed to get you thinking about who you were, who you are, and who you want to become. As you consider these questions, I want you to carefully consider the ramifications of past, present, and future decisions. This exercise cannot be accomplished in a few moments or hours. In fact, I trust the weightiness of your answers will cause you to think and rethink your responses again and again.

My Past

1. What did you want to be when you were a child? Teenager? Young adult? How did those dreams turn out?

2. List the major events that took place during your formative years that have contributed to how things turned out. These things could be major moves, the loss of a friend or loved one, the addition of a friend or loved one: something that changed the course of your life. How many of those events did you have control over?

3. What were the defining moments in your early business career (those things within five to ten years of graduating high school), that have shaped who you have become?

4. List the events you would have changed and how you would have changed them if you had the power to do so during this early period in your life.

My Present

1. Are you satisfied with who you are today? Why or why not?

2. In your own words, list a few of the things that you would like to change about your current life.

3. Would you consider your life a success? Why or why not?

4. How would you define success?

5. In all the relationships you must nurture and be aware of, which ones are the most important and why?

6. What can you add or take away from your current life schedule/routine to further enhance the relationships that are most important to you?

My Future

1. Based on the current track of your life, where will you be in five years? Ten years? Twenty years?

2. Are you satisfied with where you are headed? Why or why not?

3. What must you do in order to direct a new outcome for your future?

4. Who needs to be involved in your life plan?

5. What skills, tools, or relationships do you need to foster in order to redirect your future?

6. What do you hope to accomplish by redirecting your future plans?

You may discover additional questions that need to be answered in the process of defining or redefining your future. Don't just think about those questions, write them down and be definitive in your approach to a new future. Taking the time to invest in this final challenge will help you build momentum in your life. It is not hard to stay busy or be active; the goal is to have activity with purpose—to do those things which contribute to the end goal you wish to reach.

A Final Challenge

Your Final Chapter

It would be easy to see the final focus for this book delve into a morbid, end-of-life exercise that is overly focused on our mortality. That is certainly not my intent, but I do wish for all of you to finish well. We will always have regrets about what could have, should have, or would have happened if. If we choose to live with that focus, our final chapter will be lonely. The hope is that we can leave the past, and all the regrets that go along with it, behind us and continue to move forward.

None of us know when the final chapter of our lives will be written. There are no guarantees when it comes to the length of our days. In the only psalm written by Moses, we are encouraged to "number our days" (Psalm 90:12). There are no "do-overs" in the game of life. We live each day and then it is gone. This is not some attempt to get us thinking about the brevity of life but to accept the challenge of living each day to the fullest.

When you get up tomorrow, begin to plan your day, your week, and your life as if this is your final chapter. It matters not if you are in the spring or the fall of life; your final chapter starts today. Developing a mind-set like this will radically alter the way you lead, treat those around you, and live your life.

The leadership titles I have shared with you in this book are not something for someone else to consider, they are for you! While you may not be able to activate all of them in your life today, you can get started today with at least one of them. Pick one of them and begin living the principles found in that chapter. Build teams, consider the future, and plan for tomorrow, but live for today. As Christian leaders, we honor God best when we do what He created us to do. You were created to lead—so do it, and do not forget your final chapter starts today.

References

Scripture references

- Holy Bible, New International Version®, NIV® Copyright ©1973, 1978, 1984, 2011 by Biblica, Inc.® Taken from BibleGateway.com.
- New American Standard Bible, Copyright © 1960, 1962, 1963, 1968, 1971, 1972, 1973, 1975, 1977, 1995 by The Lockman Foundation. Published in La Habra, CA.

Chapter 1

[1] Greenleaf, R. *Servant Leadership: A Journey into the Nature and Legitimate Power and Greatness.* New York, Paulist Press. 1977, page 7

Chapter 5

[2] Burke, W. W. *Organization Change: Theory and Practice (2nd ed.).* Los Angeles, CA: Sage Publications. 2008, page 194

[3] Gladwell, M. *The Tipping Point: How Little Things Can Make a Big Difference.* NY: Little, Brown, and Company. 2002, pgs. 176-179

Chapter 6

[4] Kouzes, J. M. & Posner, B. Z. *The Leadership Challenge (4th ed.)*. San Francisco, CA: John Wiley & Sons Inc. 2007, page 29

Chapter 9

[5] Stoltzfus, T. *Leadership Coaching: The Disciplines, Skills, and Heart of a Christian Coach.* Virginia Beach, VA: Stoltzfus. 2005, page vii

[6] Stoltzfus, T. *Leadership Coaching: The Disciplines, Skills, and Heart of a Christian Coach.* Virginia Beach, VA: Stoltzfus. 2005, page 258

www.ingramcontent.com/pod-product-compliance
Lightning Source LLC
Chambersburg PA
CBHW071026240526
45469CB00006BD/2102